Oregon
SALTWATER
FISHING GUIDE

Written by Frank Haw and Raymond M. Buckley with fish fillet and skinning sections by Nick Pasquale.

Feature section by Stan Jones. Oregon map section by Milt Guymon and Harold C. Smith.

EDITOR AND PUBLISHER: Oregon Saltwater Fishing Guide is edited and published by Stanley N. Jones, Stan Jones Publishing, Inc. Business office is 3421 E. Mercer St., Seattle, Wash. 98112, phone (206) 323-3970.

ASSOCIATE PUBLISHER: Betty Lou Jones.
STAN JONES PUBLISHING, INC., Is publisher of WASHINGTON STATE FISHING GUIDE (6th ed. $8.95 pp), PACIFIC NORTHWEST SEAFOOD COOKERY ($8.95 pp), SALTWATER FISHING IN WASHINGTON ($9.95 pp), THE OREGON SALTWATER FISHING GUIDE ($9.95 pp), BRITISH COLUMBIA FISHING GUIDE ($8.50 pp). All U.S. Funds.
Printed in the United States of America
ISBN 0-939936-03-8

table of contents

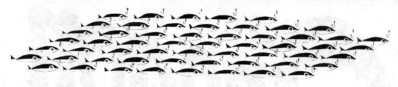

salt-water fishes
important to
northwest
anglers

The beginning pages of almost any fish book include labeled diagrams of fish. Although our approach emphasizes natural color and body form, we must concede that fish identification is simpler if one knows and uses the names of a few anatomical structures. Usually our attempts to identify a fish from a description of a curious angler, who is unfamiliar with basic fish anatomy, has been mutually frustrating. We do remember one successful telephone conversation with an excited woman. She told of catching a very strange fish:

"It was the size and shape of a throw-rug, but it had legs!"

In this case the description was adequate. The lady had obviously caught a large male skate. The "legs" were simply large paired male reproductive organs or claspers.

A fish's fins are an obvious part of its anatomy and are very useful in identification. The pelvic (ventral) and pectoral fins are paired, meaning there is one of each on the left and right side. Pectoral fins correspond to the front legs in higher vertebrates (the arms in man) and the ventral fins the rear legs (man's legs). The other fins (dorsal, caudal, and anal) are located along the midline of the fish and are not paired even though they may be subdivided into two or more separate structures, one in back of the other. Fin rays are the structures that support fin membranes. They may be hard with sharp pointed ends (spiny) or they may be soft and branched at the fin's outer edge.

4

salmon anatomy

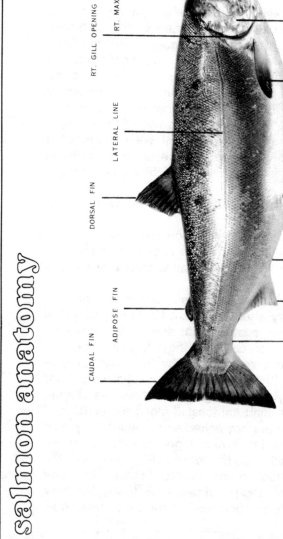

RT. GILL OPENING

RT. MAXILLARY

RT. GILL COVER

RT. PECTORAL FIN

LATERAL LINE

DORSAL FIN

RT. PELVIC FIN

ANUS

CAUDAL FIN

ADIPOSE FIN

ANAL FIN

CAUDAL PEDUNCLE

salmon anatomy 5

(Figure 1)

Salmon are typical of fish with only soft fin rays. They also have a fin with no rays — the adipose (fatty) fin. Skeletal structures of soft rayed fishes tend to be much softer than in fishes with spiny fin rays and the former are considered more primitive.

Hatchery salmon and trout are frequently fin-clipped for latter identification in the wild. Also, the maxillary bones may be clipped. To accurately report a marked fish, one must examine all of these structures for multiple fin marks and be able to distinguish a fish's right from its left.

rockfish anatomy

(Figure 2)

Rockfish are typical of fish with both spiny and soft fin rays. Although the dorsal fin of the rockfish is deeply "notched", it is a single continuous fin. Other fishes, such as cods and some sculpins, have more than one dorsal fin. These are called, beginning with the fin furthest forward, the first, second, or even the third dorsal fin.

flounder anatomy

(Figure 3)

Flounders also have both spiny and soft fin rays, but because of their unusual shape and "blind" side, their anatomy is more confusing. A flounder's mouth slants back toward its belly. The pelvic fins are located on the abrupt ridge of the belly and the anus (remarkably far forward) is just in front of the long anal fin.

6

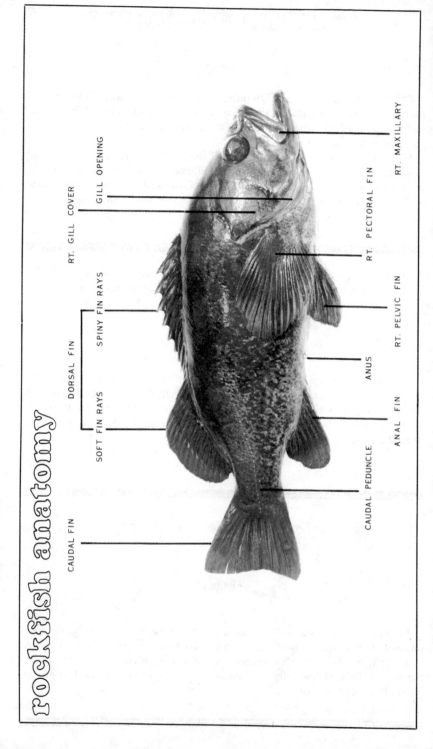

rockfish anatomy

CAUDAL FIN

SOFT FIN RAYS

DORSAL FIN

SPINY FIN RAYS

RT. GILL COVER

GILL OPENING

CAUDAL PEDUNCLE

ANAL FIN

ANUS

RT. PELVIC FIN

RT. PECTORAL FIN

RT. MAXILLARY

flounder anatomy

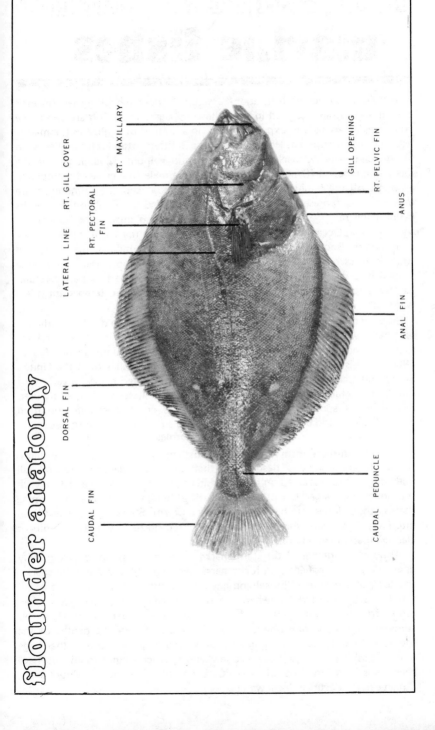

CAUDAL FIN

DORSAL FIN

LATERAL LINE   RT. GILL COVER

RT. MAXILLARY

RT. PECTORAL FIN

GILL OPENING

RT. PELVIC FIN

ANUS

ANAL FIN

CAUDAL PEDUNCLE

most frequently caught
marine fishes

Fifty-one species of fish, about a sixth of those inhabiting Northwest's coastal waters, are pictured in the following pages. These fish are about the only ones an angler can expect to hook in a lifetime of angling in the marine waters of the Northwest. However, we have omitted entire local families, such as the eel-like pricklebacks (Stichaeidae) and eelpouts (Zoarcidae); or the facinating pipefish (Syngnathidae), featuring a male that carries the young in a pouch. All the families that we have considered, except the Salmonidae, are only partially represented. The species not included either inhabit the depths beyond the range of sport gear, don't bite, are too small to be hooked, or they are rare. Occasionally, a popular sport fish from the south appears in our cool waters. Bonito have been taken in British Columbia salmon nets and white seabass have been hooked off Ilwaco and Westport. Recently a large striped bass was taken in Puget Sound, but all of these fishes are rare and usually appear in late summer or fall when our water temperatures are warmest.

Since natural color and body form are often distorted in death, mostly live specimens were photographed. The common and scientific names used are those recommended in American Fisheries Society Special Publication No. 2, 1960, "A List of Common and Scientific Names of Fishes from the United States and Canada". In addition to these recommended names, a variety of others are included under "aliases". In many cases aliases are frequently used misnomers — some of the most inappropriate are enclosed in quotation marks. Scale of grid used in fish pictures is two square inches per square.

SHARKS (Squaliformes)

The typical shark form is familiar to most anglers: an elongate body that is round in cross-section, fleshy fins that are not collapsible, several gill openings, a mouth located on the underside of the head, and a caudal fin with the upper half larger than the lower half; although in the faster swimming sharks, these lobes of the tail are more uniform. Shark eggs are fertilized internally and male sharks can be easily recognized by their prominent claspers used in copulation.

Although a number of different sharks occur in our waters, only the spiny dogfish is taken frequently. A few others, such as the blue and soupfin sharks, are occasionally hooked by salmon anglers along the outer coast. The sixgill (mud) shark, reported (elsewhere) to reach a length of 26 feet, was taken rather frequently on dogfish set lines from inner Puget Sound when this commercial fishery flourished. These giants are still in the depths of the sound and can be taken on a line baited with a dogfish or some other large morsel. Basking sharks, reported (elsewhere) to reach lengths to 45 feet, have been observed in coastal waters. Even the notorious white shark ("man-eater") occurs in local waters.

SPINY DOGFISH (Squalus acanthias) (Figure 1)
Aliases: Dogfish, "sand shark", "mud shark".
Habitat: Very abundant in sand and mud bottom areas.

Baits: Herring and other fishes — an indiscriminate feeder.

Table value: Occasionally tolerated by a few liberal sport fishermen. The flesh should be soaked overnight in a weak acid solution (a little vinegar or lemon juice in water) to remove the urea.

Figure 1, Spiny Dogfish

Most salt-water anglers are contemptuously familiar with this shark. In the past, they have been utilized as sources of sandpaper (skins), with oil and vitamin A extracted from the livers. A frayed, hookless leader is usually indication of a dogfish bite and it is wise to re-tie a hook after a dogfish bites a nylon leader. Nevertheless, introductions to dogfish have thrilled many novice salt-water anglers. The forward edges of both dorsal fins have sharp spines capable of inflicting painful and slightly venomous wounds. The WCSDC* record is 13 lb. 14 oz.

*Washington Council of Skin Diving Clubs

SKATE FAMILY (Rajidae)

Skates are closely related to sharks. They have skeletons of cartilage, several gill openings, a shark-like skin, their eggs are fertilized internally and the males have prominent claspers. Skates, however, are flat but not in the same manner as flounders; skates lie on their bellies, but flounders lie on their sides. Skate "wings" are actually modified pectoral fins. Skates are harmless, although some people confuse them with stingrays (a related fish having a dangerous spine near the tail) that are not found in the Northwest. However, a few electric rays have been taken from our waters by commercial trawlers from deep water.

SKATES (Raja sp.) (Figure 2)
Alias: "Sting ray"
Habitat: Common on muddy bottomed and in some sandy areas.
Baits: Herring, clams.
Table value: Skate "wings" are highly valued in Europe and by Oriental Americans. The wings are cut from the body, the dark side skinned, then cut into pieces and either boiled or fried. When fried, the meat resembles scallop in taste and texture.

Northwest anglers are likely to encounter three kinds of skates: big, long nose, and the starry skate (pictured here). Skates are unimpressive when hooked. They are not uncommon in catches from the ocean surf. The WCSDC record for big skate is 78 pounds 6 ounces, but they are known to attain weights of 200 pounds.

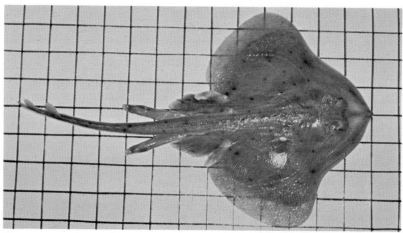

Figure 2, Starry Skate   See previous page.

CHIMAERA FAMILY (Chimaerdae)

The chimaeras are similar to the sharks and skates in having skeletons of cartilage, fins that are not collapsible, eggs that are internally fertilized, and males with claspers. They differ in having a single gill opening, a smooth skin, and a body tapering back to a pointed tail.

RATFISH (Hydrolagus colliei) (Figure 3)

Alias: Chimaera.

Habitat: Commonly taken from sandy bottomed areas in depths over 70 feet.

Baits: Most appear to be taken on herring, but there may be more effective baits.

Table value: Poor.

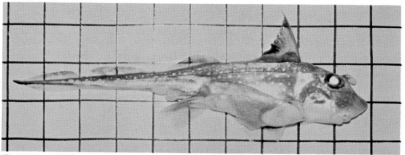

Figure 3, Ratfish

If nothing else, the appearance of a hooked ratfish provides a bizarre interlude to an outing. The forward edge of the first dorsal fin has a sharp spine capable of inflicting a painful and venomous wound. The specimen pictured is a male and differs externally from the female in possessing the head "horn" as well as claspers. Anglers outside the Pacific Northwest seldom see a chimaera. A fine odorless lubricating oil for saltwater reels, guns, and other equipment can be simply rendered from ratfish livers by placing them in a pan in a warm oven. This oil can then be poured off into a container for future use.

STURGEON FAMILY (Acipenseridae)

These are primitive fishes and shark-like in appearance. The upper half of their tail is longer than the lower half and the mouth is located on the underside of the head. Sturgeon differ from sharks in having a sucker-like toothless mouth preceded by a row of four barbels ("whiskers"), a single gill opening, and five rows of bony plates protecting their body.

Sturgeon are slow growing, long lived, and by far the largest local fishes occurring in fresh water. Both our local species also occur in salt water but as with other members of the family, spawning occurs in fresh water. Sturgeon (Huso huso), weighing 2,700 pounds, have been taken in Russia.

WHITE STURGEON (Acipenser transmontanus)

Alias: Sturgeon

Habitat: Frequents the bottom of the deeper pools and channels of the Columbia and Snake Rivers. Apparently avoids artificial reservoirs. Occasionally taken from other large coastal rivers.

Baits: Smelt, herring, larval lampreys, night crawlers.

Table value: Excellent.

A white sturgeon taken from salt water by a local angler is a rarity. A specimen weighing 1,285 lbs. was taken from the Columbia River at Vancouver in 1912. An 1,800 pounder has been reported from the Fraser River.

GREEN STURGEON (Acipenser medirostris)

Alias: Sturgeon

Habitat: Principally a salt-water fish that is most common near and in the lower estuaries of the Columbia River and some other coastal rivers. During periods of high run-off, green sturgeon appear to move away from the river mouths. These sturgeon apparently spend little time in fresh water and ascend rivers only a short distance to spawn.

Baits: Ghost shrimp, crabs, clams, and small flounders have been found in the stomachs of green sturgeon. Herring and smelt should also work.

Table value: Excellent smoked although inferior to fresh white sturgeon.

Anglers, fishing on the bottom with proper bait, should be able to take green sturgeon during the summer and early fall. Occasionally one is taken by a salmon angler using herring bait. Greens reach a weight of about 350 lbs.

Our two sturgeon species can be distinguished by the bands of olive green running the length of the green sturgeon's body, whereas whites tend to be gray above and white below. In addition, greens have 30 or fewer bony plates in the row extending along the middle of their side, in contrast to a white's 38 or more.

HERRING FAMILY (Clupeidae)

Members of this family, which includes the sardines, are of great importance to anglers as bait and forage for sport fish but one 'herring", the American shad, is itself a splendid game fish. The herrings are all schooling fishes that can be readily identified by their silvery sides, single dorsal fin, soft-rayed fins, and their lack of an adipose fin.

AMERICAN SHAD (Alosa sapidissima) (Figure 4)

Alias: Shad.

Habitat: Little is known about the marine distribution of shad off the Pacific Northwest Coast.

Lures: Rarely taken by anglers in the marine environment. Caught in fresh water on a variety of very small, bright and metallic-colored lures.

Table value: Good, if properly prepared or canned. Shad roe is generally considered a delicacy.

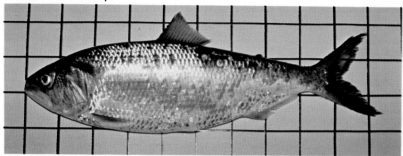

Figure 4, American Shad

Shad spawn in rivers, the females depositing small eggs that drift with the current. Shad are the only abundant local marine fish that are not native to our coast. Our shad resulted from introductions into the Sacramento and Columbia Rivers in 1871 from the East Coast. The Columbia River hosts a large shad run and smaller runs occur in other coastal rivers. Shad ascend the Columbia River in late spring, but the best angling is in June and July. The average weight of adult Columbia River shad is about 3 1/2 pounds and the maximum is about 8 pounds. However, shad to 13 1/2 pounds have been recorded elsewhere. Shad are splendid sport fish and when hooked, appear to be about as strong and fast as trout and salmon.

PACIFIC HERRING (Clupea pallasii) (Figure 5 Bottom)

Alias: Herring

Habitat: Seasonally abundant throughout much of Pacific Northwest waters. Spawning typically occurs during the winter and early spring in shallow water. The adhesive eggs are spawned onto eel grass and other seaweeds where they may be exposed at low tide.

Lures: Taken on bare hooks by jigging.

Table value: Excellent when pickled.

Herring are very familiar to anglers as the principal bait for salmon and other marine fishes. A useful method for collecting herring, however, is by "jigging" which could be considered a form of angling. Large (8-12 inch) herring doubtlessly could be taken on small flies cast into schools feeding on the surface. The maximum length of Pacific herring is reported to be 13 inches.

SMELT FAMILY (Osmeridae) (Figure 5 Top)

Smelt are small unspotted, silvery fishes with only soft-rayed fins and an adipose fin. Although several species of smelt occur in our waters, only the surf smelt is taken in saltwater on hook and line.

SURF SMELT (Hypomesus pretiosus)

Alias: Silver smelt

Habitat: Little is known about the offshore distribution of surf smelt. They regularly occur in certain areas and spawn on specific gravel beaches.

Lures: Usually taken by "jigging".

Table value: Excellent — usually fried.

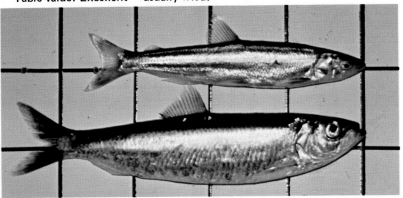

Figure 5, Pacific Herring (bottom) and Surf Smelt (top)

Smelt are taken by jigging from piers and floats principally during late winter. The average length of surf smelt is about 8 inches and the maximum about 10 inches.

Smelt dipping, with special nets, is popular during the summer months at certain beaches on the coast. The smelt are dipped as they come into the very shallow water to spawn during an approximately two-hour period before and after high tide.

Scale of grid used in fish pictures is two square inches per square.

salmon salmon

SALMON FAMILY (Salmonidae)

This is the most well known group of fishes to local anglers. All five North American species of Pacific salmon are abundant in our marine waters and spawn in Northwest streams. A sixth species of Pacific salmon, the masu salmon (Oncorhynchus masu), occurs along the Asiatic coat of the North Pacific with the five other species. All of the Northwest's native trout and char also occur in salt water as well as in fresh water.

The members of the salmon family occurring in saltwater all spawn in freshwater. Typically, these fish return to their natal streams and spawn in a nest dug in clean gravel by the female. Pacific salmon and Dolly Varden are fall spawners while steelhead and cutthroat are classed as spring spawners. Pacific salmon die after spawning, but trout (Salmo sp.) and char (Salvelinus sp.) may not.

The predominant salt-water colors of members of the salmon family are silvery sides, a white underside, and a dark, usually spotted, back. The fins of these fishes are supported only by soft rays and they all have an adipose fin. The smelts, which are closely related to salmon and trout, also have an adipose fin but smelt are unspotted small fishes that are taken by "jigging" and netting rather than by normal angling.

Pacific Salmon can be separated from trout by counting the soft rays in the anal fin. A count of the unbranched bases of the anal fin rays will be less than 12 for trout and char and 12 or more for Pacific salmon. In addition, the tail fins of trout appear more "square" and catchable sized salmon have dark pigment inside their mouths but the insides of the mouths of the trout are essentially white. Dolly Varden are the only local marine salmonoids with light colored spots on their backs and sides.

CHINOOK SALMON (Oncorhynchus tshawytscha) (Figure 6)

Aliases: King, blackmouth, spring, tyee
Habitat: See page 90.
Baits and lures: See page 54.
Table value: Excellent.

Figure 6, Chinook Salmon

Chinook salmon are the largest of the six species of Pacific salmon. A giant of 126 pounds, caught commercially in Alaska, is the largest on record and a 92-pounder from the Skeena River, British Columbia, is the largest sport-caught fish.

Chinook spawn in our large unspoiled streams from late summer to late fall. The time of upstream spawning migration varies with the race of fish and extends from February through October in the Northwest. Typically, the large glacial or colder river systems host spring runs of chinook and in the longer river systems these fish typically utilize the head waters for spawning. Later "running" fish typically spawn nearer the sea. Although there are some remarkable exceptions, male chinook usually mature at ages 2 to 5 while females mature at age 4 or 5. The young of late run or "fall chinook" usually migrate to sea during the first spring of life, while the young of early running fish or "spring chinook" usually spend a year in fresh water before migrating to sea. Most of the fish weighing 40 pounds or more taken in the Northwest appear to be in at least their fifth year of life.

Mature 2-year-old male chinook are called "jacks". Chinook showing no signs of sexual maturity are sometimes called "blackmouth" while larger fish, those showing signs of sexual maturity, are called "kings". As chinook salmon approach sexual maturity, their scales become more firmly imbedded and their predominant color changes from silver to various shades of brown. As with all Pacific salmon, the maturing male develops a hook snout, large canine teeth, and "razor- back".

The runs of Northwest chinook salmon have been greatly enhanced by artificial production and, due to the continuing losses of our natural fresh-water environment, the future of chinook angling along the coast doubtlessly depends on continuing and accelerated hatchery programs.

COHO SALMON (Oncorhynchus kisutch) (Figure 7)

Aliases: Silver, hooknose.
Habitat: See page 90.
Baits and lures: See page 54.
Table value: Excellent.

Figure 7, Coho Salmon

In terms of numbers of salmon caught in recent years, coho have comprised about 60 per cent of the Northwest's salmon sport catch. Northwest coho salmon usually mature at 3 years of age, although sexually precocious 2-year-old males ("jacks") are common in hatchery runs. Coho salmon spawn in virtually all of our small, unspoiled lowland streams. Adult coho typically enter their natal streams with the October freshets and spawn in November and December; however, there are some notable exceptions. Most Columbia River coho enter the main stem in early September and spawn the following month. Young coho typically spend a full year in fresh water, migrating to sea during the spring of their second year of life. Since these young coho rear in the smaller streams, the ultimate survival of wild coho depends upon adequate stream flows during this early fresh-water existence. Since the coho fishing at any one time is dependent on a single age group of fish, a dry summer can damage coho fishing for an entire season.

The local coho population has been greatly supplemented by artificial hatchery production in recent years. Nowhere is this more evident than in the booming sport fishery at the mouth of the Columbia River.

The record coho is a 31-pound fish taken by an angler at Cowichan Bay, Vancouver Island, B.C.. The largest Washington sport-caught coho recorded is a 26 pound fish taken at Westport, Washington. Nearly all of the catches of big "silvers" (more than 20 pounds) that biologists are asked to verify are

16

actually chinook salmon lacking tail spotting, but these fish always possess the black lower gumline. Largest coho usually are found late in the season. Washington's Chehalis River system, for instance, hosts large fish, some in the 20-pound-plus class.

PINK SALMON (Oncorhynchus gorbuscha) (Figure 8)
Aliases: Humpback salmon, humpie.

Habitat: See page 90.
Baits and lures: See page 54.
Table value: Excellent.

Figure 8, Pink Salmon

The large, cold river systems of (Nisqually, Puyallup) Puget Sound are essentially the southern extremity of the pink salmon's North American spawning range. However, a few occasionally appear in streams as far south as the Sacramento River, California. Spawning pink salmon are 2 year olds. Many streams in northern British Columbia and Alaska have even year runs. Local pink salmon typically spawn in October and the young leave the stream during the early spring of the following year soon after emerging from spawning gravel. The spawning colors of pink salmon are brownish above with white on lower sides and belly. The maximum weight for this species appears to be about 15 pounds with large fish most evident in years of poor abundance.

CHUM SALMON (Oncorhynchus keta) (Figure 9)
Aliases: Dog salmon, fall salmon
Habitat: Adult chum salmon apparently move quickly through our coastal waters from their feeding areas in the North Pacific.

Baits and lures: Occasionally taken by salmon anglers on herring and herring-strip baits.
Table value: Excellent — especially when smoked or kippered.
In recent years, up to two thousand chum salmon have been taken annually by Washington marine anglers. They are rather common in fall sport catches at Point No Point, Hood Canal, southern Puget Sound, and in the Chehalis River. Large hook-and-line catches (floating set lines) have been made in North Pacific by the Japanese using salted anchovies for bait. Up until the 1940's, there was a specific sport fishery for chum at Gig Harbor, near Tacoma. These anglers primarily used herring-strip baits. Chum salmon populations have undergone a serious decline throughout the southern portion of their North American range.

Typically, chum spawn in the late fall rather close to salt water. Soon after

Figure 9, Chum Salmon

emerging from the gravel, the young migrate to sea. Local runs are comprised primarily of three, four, and five-year- old fish. The spawning colors of chum salmon are predominantly olive with streaks of red and yellow. The maximum weight of chum salmon is about 33 pounds.

SOCKEYE SALMON (Oncorhynchus nerka) (Figure 10)

Aliases: Red salmon (Alaska), blue back (Columbia and Quinault Rivers). Kokanee or "silver trout" are names used for the land-locked form.

Habitat: Like chum salmon, adult sockeye apparently move quickly through our coastal waters from their feeding areas in the North Pacific.

Table value: Excellent — most of the catch is canned.

Figure 10, Sockeye Salmon

Although millions of these salmon migrate through our marine waters annually, only a few hundred are taken by anglers. However, as with chum salmon, Japanese floating set lines have taken large numbers of sockeye in the North Pacific. Canadian commercial trollers have also begun to catch sockeye off the west coast of Vancouver Island using flashers and small plastic squid-like lures. In Alaska, sea-run sockeye are important sport fish in streams where they are taken on various artificial lures.

Sockeye typically spawn in tributaries to lakes but they also utilize certain gravelly beaches in the lakes. The young usually spend a year rearing in a lake before migrating to sea. Sockeye mature primarily in from 3 to 5 years. Their maximum weight is about 15 pounds. The spawning colors of sockeye are red on back and sides and a greenish head.

Landlocked sockeye salmon (kokanee) are very important to local anglers and are stocked in many lakes in and outside of their natural range. These fish spend their entire lives within a lake system area. Like other Pacific salmon, kokanee die after spawning.

STEELHEAD (RAINBOW) TROUT (Salmo gairdneri) (Figure 11)

Aliases: Steelhead — a sea-run rainbow trout. The term rainbow trout is used for fresh water forms.

Habitat: Steelhead apparently spend most of their marine lives well offshore in the North Pacific. They appear to be on spawning and post-spawning migrations when taken by marine anglers.

Lures: Most steelhead taken from salt-water are caught on artificial spoons and "bobbers". In addition, a few are taken incidentally on various types of salmon lures.

Table value: Excellent.

Figure 11, Steelhead Trout   Stan Jones Photo

Steelhead typically first mature in their third, fourth, or fifth year of life. The young fish spend two or three years in the stream before migrating to sea. However, hatchery-reared steelhead are released at migratory size after one year in fresh water and these fish return predominantly as 3-year-olds. Although steelhead trout are capable of spawning more than once, they apparently suffer high post-spawning mortalities and returns are predominantly comprised of initial spawners.

The Northwest sport catch is primarily dependent upon fish entering the streams during the winter months but some rivers, notably the Columbia system, also contain larger numbers of summer and spring-run fish. These fish, as well as winter run steehead, spawn during the late winter-early spring period. Like spring chinook, they store considerable amounts of body fats for sustenance in fresh water.

The world record steelhead trout is a 42-pounder from Southeast Alaska.

Scale of grid used in fish pictures is two square inches per square.

CUTTHROAT TROUT (Salmo clarki) (Figure 12)

Aliases: Sea-run cutthroat, sea-run, cutthroat, harvest trout, "blueback".

Habitat: Occurs in virtually all of our large and small unspoiled coastal streams. Sea-run forms are present within the inter-tidal zones (between the low and high tide marks) in most of our marine areas.

Baits and lures: Spoons, spinners, small cut bait from herring, sandlance, and sculpin bellies, salmon roe.

Table value: Good.

Figure 12, Cutthroat Trout

Cutthroat trout exhibit remarkable variation, principally in color and spotting, throughout their natural range so that it is far easier to distinguish Yellowstone cutthroat from coastal cutthroat than it is coastal cutthroat from rainbow (steelhead) trout. Coastal cutthroat often lack the red "cutthroat marks" on either side of the lower jaw. Mature "sea-runs" usually range between 10 and 20 inches in length — anything larger is an exceptional fish. The largest specimens are from lakes. A cutthroat weighing over 40 pounds was once taken from Pyramid Lake, Neveda. The maximum size for "sea-runs" is about 5 lbs.

Cutthroat trout are late winter-early spring spawners, although "sea-runs" typically ascend rivers from late summer through fall. Most slat-water-caught cutthroat are taken within the inter-tidal zone.

Scale of grid used in fish pictures is two square inches per square.

DOLLY VARDEN (Salvelinus malma) (Figure 13)

Aliases: Dolly Varden trout, Dolly, bull trout.

Habitat: Typically occur in colder river systems (of glacial origin) and associated deep lakes. Sea-run fish occur in and near the estuaries of Dolly Varden streams, frequently in the inter-tidal zone.

Bait and lures: A good "spoon" and plug fish but also taken on salmon roe in both fresh and salt water.

Table value: Excellent.

Figure 13, Dolly Varden

The Dolly Varden is the only member of the salmon family found in salt water that has light colored spots on its back and sides. All other members of the family have dark colored spots. Sea-run Dolly Varden typically ascend local streams in mid-summer and spawn in the streams in the fall. Mature sea-run fish usually range from 15-25 inches in length. (The specimen pictured, a male, is exceptionally large for a sea-run fish.) Lake and reservoir-reared fish attain the largest size, with the record being a 32-pound specimen from Lake Pend Oreille, Idaho. Most of the marine-caught Dollies are taken within the inter-tidal zone.

CODFISH AND HAKE FAMILY (Gadidae)

Members of this family are elongated, round-bodied fishes usually having three dorsal and two anal fins. The fins of these fishes lack spines. Although the Pacific hake is included in this family, its second dorsal fin and single anal fin are only deeply "notched", but hake appear to have the standard codfish fin counts. Some scientists include hake in a different but closely related family (Merlucciidae). The burbot ("fresh-water lingcod"), the only fresh-water member of the cod family, occurs in certain Northwest lakes in the upper Columbia River system. This same fish is also found in certain lakes in Europe, northern Asia, and else where in northern North America. The burbot is closely related to the European ling (Molva sp.) rather than to saltwater lingcod (Ophiodon elongatus).

PACIFIC COD (Gadus macrocephalus) (Figure 14, Middle)

Aliases: Cod, true cod.

Habitat: A schooling, moving fish usually found near a smooth, firm bottom in more than 80 feet of water. It is especially abundant from winter through early spring in coastal waters.

Bait and lures: Herring, metal jigs.

Table value: Excellent, usually filleted and fried.

Pacific cod, like many of our other deep-water fish, are dull when hooked, but they are fine food fish. Most skilled cod anglers take them on plain metal jigs. The cod attain weights of more than 20 lbs. in local waters and have been taken over 40 pounds in Alaska. Pacific cod can be distinguished from walleye pollock in that the former possesses a prominent barbel (whisker) and an upper jaw that extends beyond the lower jaw.

PACIFIC TOMCOD (Microgadus proximus) (Figure 14, Top)

Aliases: Tomcod, (small) cod.

Habitat: A migrating schooling fish, abundant during the summer months in coastal harbors and bays. They are often taken around piers and floats.

Bait: Indiscriminate feeders.

Table value: Good, although too small to fillet.

Tomcod are too small to interest most anglers, but they do provide good sport for youngsters. The maximum length is about 12 inches. Pacific tomcod can be distinguished from small Pacific cod in that the latter has a larger barbel (whisker) and its anus is directly under its second, rather than its first, dorsal fin.

WALLEYE POLLOCK (Theragra chalcogrammus) (Figure 14, Bottom)

Aliases: Cod, popeye.

Habitat: A moving, schooling fish usually found near bottom in depths over 75 feet.

Bait: Herring

Table value: Fair, although quite soft and often heavily parasitized.

These fish have little to offer anglers. They are seldom available to youngsters on piers and are most often discarded when caught by boat fishermen. The maximum length is about three feet.

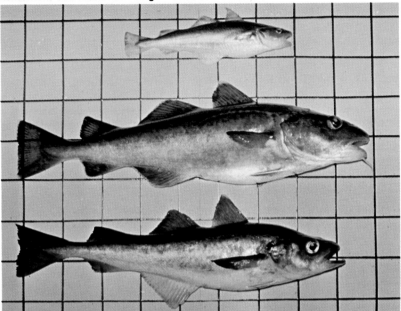

Figure 14, Pacific Cod (middle), Pacific Tomcod (top), Walleye Pollock (bottom)

These fish have little to offer anglers. They are seldom available to youngsters on piers and are most often discarded when caught by boat fishermen. The maximum length is about three feet.

PACIFIC HAKE (Merluccius productus) (Figure 15)

Alias: Hake.

Habitat: A schooling, moving fish usually found over a smooth bottom in water deeper than 150 feet. Pacific hake may be abundant just off bottom or on the surface — the latter situation frequently occurs at night.

Bait: Herring.

Table value: Good, although they will become soft if not cleaned and cooled quickly.

Figure 15, Pacific Hake

From an angler's viewpoint, the most exciting thing about hake is that they leave a salmon-like bite mark on a herring bait. In recent years, Pacific hake have been exploited heavily off the Northwest coast primarily by Russian trawlers. The Russians process these fish quickly and freeze them for later human consumption. The Pacific hake taken by American fishermen are primarily reduced for animal food. In late winter and early spring hake are concentrated in coastal bays and harbors where they are heavily exploited by local trawlers. The maximum length of hake is reported to be three feet but most are much smaller.

SURFPERCH FAMILY (Embiotocidae)

The surfperches are rather small, flat-sided fishes with fins supported by both sharp spines and soft rays. Their pectoral fins are long, delicate and semi-transparent. Although many other fishes bear live young, this family is remarkable in that prior to birth the young are nourished through a placental-type structure rather than with nutrients contained within the egg. The surfperches are fine sport fish.

REDTAIL SURFPERCH (Amphistichus rhodoterus) (Figure 16, Bottom)

Aliases: Seaperch, perch, redtails.

Habitat: Abundant in the surf along ocean beaches.

Baits and lures: Razor clam parts, mussels, shrimp, ghost shrimp, shore crabs, small polychaete worms, small spoons.

Table value: Good. Difficult to fillet — best cleaned and fried with skin on. Bones and skin are easily removed after cooking.

Figure 16, Redtail Surfperch (bottom), Striped Seaperch (top)

This is an important ocean beach surf fish. They are attractive, scrappy, and will take a variety of natural baits as well as small wobbling spoons. Redtails are not exploited by local commercial fishermen and are very abundant in some areas. The maximum length of these fish is about 16 inches.

STRIPED SEAPERCH (Embiotoca lateralis) (Figure 16, Top)

Aliases: Blue perch, perch

Habitat: Occurs in shallow waters during the late spring through early winter months throughout Washington's Puget Sound and in protected bays along the outer coast. Apparently retreats to deeper waters during the late winter through early spring months. Prefers areas with profuse growths of barnacles and mussels as well as eelgrass beds.

Baits: Polychaetous worms, shrimp, ghost shrimp, mussels, and shore crabs.

Table value: Same as redtail surfperch.

One of the most attractive local fishes. Often visible grazing among pier pilings with heavy cultures of mussels and barnacles. A fine little fish with surprising speed and strength. Striped seaperch are selective feeders, often rejecting a baited hook after close examination. They are best taken on a light leader, light sinker and a small hook (a size No. 4 is recommended). Striped seaperch and pileperch can sometimes by "chumed" (attracted into biting) by scraping barnacles and mussels loose from a piling. The maximum length is about 15 inches.

PILE PERCH (Rhacochilus vacca) (Figure 17)

Aliases: Silver perch, perch

Habitat: Similar to the striped seaperch, however, it apparently is more of a moving, schooling fish and is often abundant in the inter-tidal zone at the heads of mud-bottomed bays.

Bait: Same as for striped seaperch.

Table value: Similar to redtail surfperch.

Figure 17, Pile Perch

The pile perch is as fine a sport fish as the striped seaperch and it grows to a larger size. Maximum length about 17 inches.

SHINER PERCH (Cymatogaster aggregata) (Figure 18)

Aliases: Yellow shiner, shiner, pogy.

Habitat: A schooling, moving fish, abundant from late spring through late fall in shallow waters. Apparently moves into deeper water in winter. Frequently observed in tight schools over shallow water, feeding on the surface.

Bait: Very indiscriminate.

Table value: Dried and pickled extensively by Oriental Americans.

Figure 18, Shiner Perch

Shiner perch are too small to interest most anglers. A small bait and hook (a No. 12 is recommended) is necessary to take them. They are a fine live bait for rockfish and occasionally are eaten by salmon. Schools of three- to seven-inch fish observed "sculling" about with their pectoral fins are usually shiner perch. Maximum length about eight inches.

ROCKFISH FAMILY (Scorpaenidae)

Rockfish are heavy-boned, spiny fishes, large through the head and "shoulders". Although they are bass-like in appearance, based on internal characteristics they are in a family separate from sea bass (Serranidae) and fresh-water "bass" (Micropterus sp.). The term "cod" is even more inappropriate for the rockfishes.

COPPER ROCKFISH (Sebastodes caurinus) (Figure 19)

Alias: "Rockcod".

Habitat: Prefers rocky bottom areas and is widely distributed along the Pacific Northwest coast. Often found in shallow water around rocks, kelp, or pilings during the summer but most frequently taken from depths greater than 50 feet.

Baits and lures: Herring, shiner perch (best live), shrimp, large polychaete worms, jigs.

Table value: Excellent, usually filleted and fried.

Figure 19, Copper Rockfish

Scale of grid used in fish pictures is two square inches per square.

QUILLBACK ROCKFISH (Sebastodes maliger) (Figure 20)

Alias: "Rockcod"

Habitat: Usually restricted to rocky bottoms below 50 feet. Can be very abundant on rocky reefs in areas of strong tidal current.

Baits and lures: Same as for copper rockfish.

Table value: Excellent tasting fish, usually filleted and fried.

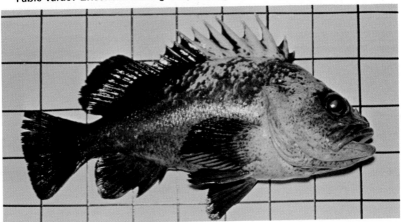

Figure 20, Quillback Rockfish

One of the most common rockfishes in sport catches. Most fishermen do not distinguish quillback from the copper rockfish, however, the former can be identified by the orange-brown (rust colored) spots of the "throat" area.

BLUE ROCKFISH (Sebastodes mystinus) (Figure 21, Top)

Aliases: "Bass", "seabass", "black seabass".

Habitat: Similar to the black rockfish.

Baits and lures: Similar to black rockfish.

Table value: Good.

Only the angler-naturalist is likely to distinguish blue from black rockfish. In the blue, the upper jaw or maxillary extends only to the middle of the eye when the mouth is closed and in the black rockfish, it extends at least to the rear edge of the eye. In addition, when the anal fin is extended on the black rockfish, its upper rear corner is in front of the lower rear corner of the fin, while in the blue, either the reverse is true or the corners are vertically in line. The blue rockfish is a very important sport fish along the central California coast. Maximum length is 21 inches.

BLACK ROCKFISH (Sebastodes melanops) (Figure 21, Bottom)

Aliases: "bass", "seabass", "black seabass"

Habitat: Abundant during summer in shallow water along the rocky kelp-lined shores of the outer coast. Apparently retreats to deeper water during late fall through early spring months.

months.

Baits and lures: Jigs, herring, and even surface plugs and flies when fish are showing on the surface.

Table value: Good, usually filleted and fried.

Figure 21, Blue Rockfish (top), Black Rockfish (bottom)

This rockfish is a fine sport fish when taken from shallow water. Large schools of black rockfish feeding on the surface are a common sight. When fishing close to shore, it is not uncommon to observe one of these fish pass by a herring bait to grab the sinker. Black rockfish prefer a moving or spinning bait or lure. These fish are apparently attracted to light and can be taken readily at night on feathered jigs.

CANARY ROCKFISH (Sebastodes pinniger) (Figure 22)

Figure 22, Canary Rockfish

Alias: "Red snapper".

Habitat: Always taken near bottom and usually in depths over 150 feet. These fish are not restricted to rocky bottom areas.

Bait and lures: Herring, large jigs.

Table value: Excellent, usually filleted and fried.

Canary rockfish are apparently deep water schooling fish associated with specific bottom locations. Since they are most often located well away from land, it is usually necessary to triangulate one's position to locate a productive area. Once this is done, fishing for these fish can be most productive. The WCSDC record is 9 lb. 10 oz.

Scale of grid used in fish pictures is two square inches per sqaure.

YELLOWEYE ROCKFISH (Sebastodes ruberrimus) (Figure 23)

Alias: "Red snapper"

Habitat: Always found near bottom, usually in depth greater than 150 feet over rocks. Occurs along the outer coast.

Bait: Herring.

Table value: Excellent, usually filleted and fried.

Figure 23, Yelloweye Rockfish

Few anglers distinguish this red rockfish from the canary rockfish (both are usually called "red snapper"), but the yelloweye can be distinguished by the black edges on its soft-rayed fins. There are no members of the snapper family (Lutjanidae) off the Northwest coast although yelloweye and canary rockfish are marketed as "red snapper". This is one of the largest of our rockfish. A yelloweye of 23 pounds has been caught.

CHINA ROCKFISH (Sebastodes nebulosus) (Figure 24)

Aliases: "Bass","rockcod".

Habitat: Common during the summer months along the outer coast off steep shorelines.

Baits and lures: Herring, jigs.

Table value: Excellent, usually filleted and fried.

China rockfish appear to inhabit the depths just below those occupied by black rockfish. They are unimpressive when hooked. The WCSDC record is 3 pounds, 7 ounces.

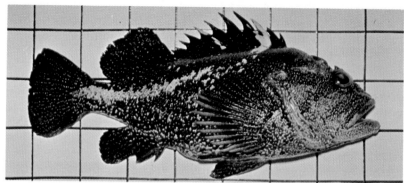

Figure 24, China Rockfish

YELLOWTAIL ROCKFISH (Sebastodes flavidus) (Figure 25)

Alias: "Bass".

Habitat: Schools of yellowtail rockfish are encountered sporadically in coastal bays. They occur more commonly in the ocean catches from offshore waters where they appear either on the bottom or near the surface.

Bait and lures: Herring, jigs.

Table value: Excellent, usually filleted and fried.

Figure 25, Yellowtail Rockfish

When near the surface, yellowtail rockfish are frequently caught by salmon fishermen. They are strong fish when hooked in shallow water. The WCSDC record is 6 pounds, 6 ounces.

WIDOW ROCKFISH (Sebastodes entomelas) (Figure 26)

Figure 26, Widow Rockfish

Aliases: "Bass", "brown bomber".

Habitat: Common in sport catches off the mouth of Columbia River.

Baits and lures: Herring, jigs.

Table value: Excellent, usually filleted and fried.

This is another of the rockfishes that is quite game when hooked.

SABLEFISH FAMILY (Anoplopomatidae)

The sablefishes are elongated, round-bodied, smooth-headed and have two dorsal fins. Their fin spines are not prickly. There are only two members of the family and one, the skilfish, is rare.

SABLEFISH (Anoplopoma fimbria) (Figure 27)

Aliases: "Blackcod", "mackerel".

Habitat: Often abundant in open waters near the surface in and around the tide rips.

Baits: Herring.

Table value: The flesh has a high oil content that results in an excellent smoked product.

Figure 27, Sablefish

Most sport-caught sablefish are caught incidentally by salmon anglers trolling or "mooching" with herring bait. They appear to be only young sablefish since they are typically small, uniform in size, and grow noticeably from winter through early fall. Although sablefish reach weights of 40 pounds, a two pounder is a good size for sport anglers. Large fish from the North Pacific have been taken from depths as great at 1,000 feet. Literature indicates a slow growth rate for sablefish.

SCULPIN FAMILY (Cottidae)

Many species of sculpins occur in local marine and fresh waters, but most are small and are seldom seen by anglers. Members of the family typically have large, flattened, horny heads having given rise to the name "bullhead". These fish, however, should not be confused with members of the fresh-water catfish family (Ictaluridae) which possess barbels ("whiskers") and an adipose fin. Sculpins have very large pectoral fins and when out of water, their body shape is such that they rest on their bellies rather than on their sides.

PACIFIC STAGHORN SCULPIN (Leptocottus armatus) (Figure 28)

Alias: Bullhead.

Habitat: Sandy and mixed sand and rock bottoms found within and just below the inter-tidal zone. Apparently avoids surf.

Baits and lures: A greedy and indiscriminate feeder. Will frequently chase an artificial lure to the surface in shallow water.

Table value: Good. Remove the head and viscera, clean and fry.

Figure 28, Pacific Staghorn Sculpin

Staghorn sculpins are common in shallow water in coastal waters where they will bury themselves in sand for cover. They have provided a great deal of recreation for youngsters and are taken in large numbers from piers and shore. The maximum length is about 12 inches.

BUFFALO SCULPIN (Enophrys bison) (Figure 29)

Alias: Bullhead.

Habitat: Similar to the Red Irish Lord, but appears to prefer shallower water and an abundance of seaweed.

Baits: Herring, crabs, mussels, polychaete worms.

Table value: Probably good, but a rather small tidbit.

Figure 29, Buffalo Sculpin

The fish are commonly taken by youngsters and are usually discarded. Their large "horns" are a remarkable characteristic.

RED IRISH LORD (Hemilepidotus hemilepidotus) (Figure 30)

Alias: Bullhead.

Habitat: Occurs on the bottom near rocks, rubble or pilings below and in the lower inter-tidal zone. Individuals from deeper water are reddish in color while those taken from shallow water are predominantly brown.

Baits: Herring, crab, mussels, polychaete worms.

Table value: Apparently good.

These fish are only occasionally taken by anglers. Maximum length is about 12 inches.

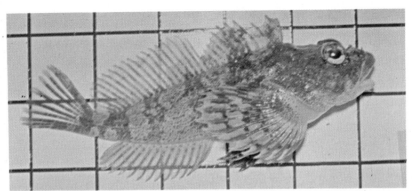

Figure 30, Red Irish Lord See previous page.

CABEZON (Scorpaenichthys marmoratus) (Figure 31)

Aliases: "Bullcod", bullhead, giant marbled sculpin.

Habitat: Occurs below and in the lower inter-tidal zone, usually on rock and sand bottoms.

Baits: Crab, live shiner perch, and live herring.

Table value: Good, usually filleted and fried. Like the lingcod, the flesh may be blue-green, but will turn white when cooked.

Warning: Cabezon roe (eggs) are reported to be poisonous.

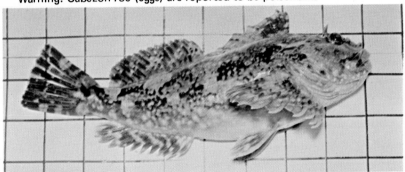

Figure 31, Cabezon

Cabezon are an important fish, by weight for the skin diving harvest. Relatively few are taken by anglers indicating that ordinary herring bait is ineffective for cabezon. The sight of a large cabezon in shallow water dashing for cover in a "cloud" of sand is always exciting. The WCSDC record is 22 pounds, 4 ounces.

GREENLING FAMILY (Hexagramidae)

The greenlings are elongated, round-bodied, often colorful fishes with no boney projections or spines on their heads. They appear to have two dorsal fins, but actually it is a single, deeply-notched fin. They have long anal fins and pectoral fins that are large and rounded.

LINGCOD (Ophiodon elongatus) (Figure 32)

Alias: "Ling".

Habitat: Frequents the depths below the inter-tidal zone among boulders, rubble, and reefs, usually in areas of strong tidal currents.

Baits and lures: Herring (best live), live greenling, flounder, rockfish, large jigs, octopus.

Table value: Excellent, usually filleted or steaked and fried. Some lingcod have blue-green bodies and flesh, but this is harmless and the flesh turns white when cooked.

Figure 32, Lingcod

Although not spectacular when hooked, the powerful rushes of lingcod for freedom through kelp and among encrusted boulders are often successful. Lingcod teeth abrade nylon. The WCSDC record is 82 pounds, 1 ounce.

KELP GREENLING (Hexagrammos decagrammus) (Figures 33, 34)

Aliases: "kelpcod", "rocktrout"
Habitat: Rocky, kelp-lined shorelines and reefs below the inter-tidal zone.

Baits and lures: Herring, polychaete worms, small jigs, shrimp.
Table value: Excellent, usually filleted and fried.

Figure 33, Male Kelp Greenling

Figure 34, Female Kelp Greenling

Kelp greenling are one of the gamier and handsome bottomfish. As noted elsewhere, they are fine bait for lingcod. The WCSDC record is 4 pounds, 10 ounces. The photographs indicate the varying color phases and the interesting difference between male and female.

WHITESPOTTED GREENLING (Hexagrammos stelleri) (Figure 35)

Aliases: "Kelpcod", "rocktrout".

Habitat: Taken near rocks, pilings, and kelp.

Baits: Mussels, polychaete worms, shrimp.

Table value: Excellent.

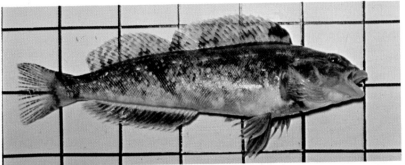

Figure 35, Whitespotted Greenling

This greenling is not common in local sport catches and those taken are usually shorter than 12 inches. The WCSDC record is 3 pounds, 8 ounces.

JACK, SCAD AND POMPANO FAMILY (Carangidae)

These are warm-water fishes and although they may resemble mackerel or tuna, they are neither. Like these swift-moving fishes, their tails are deeply forked and their caudal peduncles are very slender. Some very important sport fishes, such as the crevalle jack and permit of the Atlantic coast and the yellowtail of California, are included in the family.

JACK MACKEREL (Trachurus symmetricus) (Figure 36)

Aliases: "Spanish mackerel", "mackerel", scad.

Habitat: A schooling fish of the open sea encountered off the Columbia River's mouth from late summer through early fall.

Baits and lures: The entire local sport catch apparently is taken accidentally on salmon tackle.

Table value: Good — commercially canned extensively in California.

Figure 36, Jack Mackerel

Jack mackerel are only transient in our coastal waters. They are strong, swift moving fish and before they are landed, anglers usually think they have hooked a salmon. The maximum length is 30 inches.

MACKEREL AND TUNA FAMILY (Scombridae)

These are beautifully streamlined, schooling fishes of the open sea. They prefer warmer waters than resident fish and occur off the Northwest coast during the late summer and fall in the off-shore "blue" water.

Mackerel and tuna have very slender, keeled caudle peduncles, a series of little fins (finlets) behind their dorsal and anal fins and their bodies are nearly round in cross section.

ALBACORE (Thunnus alalunga) (Figure 37)

Alias: Tuna.

Habitat: Occur during the summer and fall in the blue oceanic waters usually found from 30 to 80 miles off the coast.

Baits and lures: In California, most are taken on live anchovies or sardines. Elsewhere, where a live bait industry has not been developed, most are taken on trolled feathered jigs. Albacore will take other lures and herring baits.

Table value: Excellent.

Figure 37, Albacore

The usual fishing procedure is to troll feathered jigs on the surface from 80 to 100 feet in back of the boat at about five knots until fish are hooked. Groups of birds in the water and surface swirling fish frequently indicate the presence of albacore. An albacore strike is spectacular and although they do not jump when hooked, and one is very much like another, they are very swift and strong. The record albacore is 93 pounds. The average weight is approximately 15 pounds.

RIGHTEYE FLOUNDER FAMILY (Pleuronectidae)

The righteye flounders typically lie on their left, or "blind", side. Newly

Figure 38, Rocksole

hatched flounders resemble other fishes, but their typical body form quickly develops and one eye "migrates" to the one side of the head.

ROCK SOLE (Lepidopsetta bilineata) (Figure 38)

Aliases: Sole, flounder.

Habitat: Found in and below the inter-tidal zone over pebbles or mixed sand and pebbly bottoms.

Baits and lures: Polychaete worms, clam parts, mussels, herring, small jigs.

Table value: Good.

Rock sole, like starry flounders, are aggressive feeders and will often follow and take an artificial spoon or fly near the surface. The skin of the rock sole is rough to the touch.

STARRY FLOUNDER (Platichthys stellatus) (Figure 39)

Alias: Flounder.

Habitat: Common on sandy or soft bottoms in and below the inter-tidal zone. Also, often in estuaries and the lower regions of coastal streams.

Baits and lures: Clam parts, mussels, polychaete worms, herring, small jigs.

Table value: Good.

Figure 39, Starry Flounder

This is one of the most important flounders in the sport catch. They are aggressive and rather indiscriminate feeders and are frequently taken on artificial lures. The maximum weight is about 20 pounds. These fish can be readily identified by their striped fins.

SAND SOLE (Psettichthys melanostictus) (Figure 40)

Aliases: Flounder, sole.

Habitat: Taken below the inter-tidal zone on sand bottoms.

Baits: Herring, clam parts, polychaete worms.

Table value: Good.

Sand sole are one of the more attractive flounders and can be identified by the several long fin rays extending beyond the fin membrane at the forward

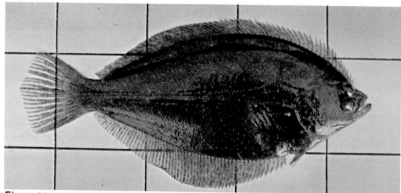

Figure 40, Sand Sole

end of their dorsal fin and their thick caudal peduncles. The maximum length is about 25 inches.

ENGLISH SOLE (Parophrys vetulus) (Figure 41)

Aliases: Flounder, sole, lemon sole.

Habitat: Occur on sand and soft bottoms below the inter-tidal zone, with the largest populations well below the reach of conventional sport gear.

Baits: Clam parts, polychaete worms.

Table value: Excellent.

Figure 41, English Sole

English sole are a valuable local commercial flounder. They are one of the more slender species of flatfish taken by anglers and their skin is relatively smooth. English sole appear to be absent from sport catches during winter months.

ARROWTOOTH FLOUNDER (Atheresthes stomias) (Figure 42)

Aliases: Flounder, turbot, bastard halibut.

Habitat: Usually taken over sand or soft bottoms at depths greater than 80 feet.

Bait: Herring.

Table value: Good, however, it becomes very soft if not filleted and cooled quickly.

This flounder can be identified by its large mouth, long sharp teeth, and relatively slender shape. Also, its scales are easily rubbed off. Arrowtooth flounder are frequently misidentified as halibut by local anglers. It is one of

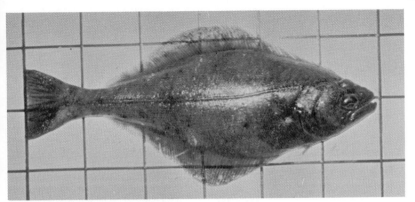

Figure 42, Arrowtooth Flounder

the larger flounders reaching a length of about 30 inches.

FLATHEAD SOLE (Hippoglossoides elassodon) (Figure 43)

Aliases: Flounder, sole.

Habitat: Common over smooth bottoms at moderate depths.

Table value: Good, although it becomes soft if not cleaned and cooled quickly.

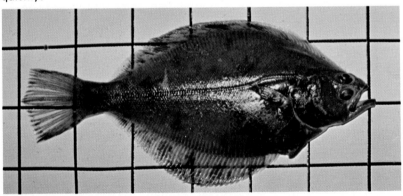

Figure 43, Flathead Sole

These fish are not important in the sport catch. They are similar to petrale in body form, but are generally smaller, have a proportionately larger head, and are softer. Their maximum length is about 18 inches.

PETRALE SOLE (Eopsetta jordani) (Figure 44)

Aliases: Flounder, sole

Habitat: Abundant off the coast in depths ranging from 180 to 1,200 feet, inhabiting deeper water in the winter than in summer.

Bait: Primarily taken by salmon anglers on herring bait.

A few petrale are taken by sport fishermen, but the large populations are well below and beyond the reach of anglers. The petrale command the highest commercial price of any flounder except halibut. The maximum weight is about seven pounds.

See next page.

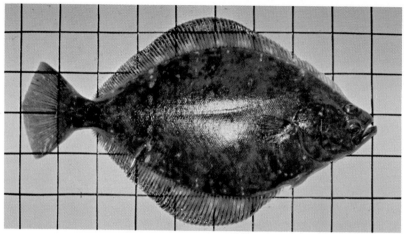

Figure 44, Petrale Sole See previous page.

C-O SOLE (Pleuronichthys coenosus) (Figure 45)
Aliases: Sole, flounder.
Table value: Good.

Figure 45 C-O Sole

These fish are uncommon in sport catches and are apparently usually below the range of conventional sport gear. Their name comes from the unusual markings on their "top side". The maximum length is 14 inches

PACIFIC HALIBUT (Hippoglossus stenolepis) (Figure 46)
Alias: Halibut.
Habitat: Occurs on sandy bottoms usually at depths greater than 75 feet in coastal bays, and throughout Juan de Fuca Strait and along the outer coast generally becoming less common to the southward.
Baits: Herring, octopus.
Table value: Excellent.

Figure 46, Pacific Halibut

Because they are so large and good to eat, Pacific halibut are probably the most highly regarded of all West coast bottom fishes. Most sport caught halibut are taken incidentally by salmon anglers. The strength of a large halibut becomes especially evident after they are boated. Knowledgeable anglers prefer to first subdue them alongside. The maximum weight is about 500 pounds.

LEFTEYE FLOUNDER FAMILY (Bothidae)

These fish are so named because they typically have their eyes on the left side of their head. Only one species enters the Northwest sport catch. The California halibut, a popular sport fish in California, is a member of this family.

PACIFIC SANDDAB (Citharichthys sordidus) (Figure 47)

Aliases: Sanddab, sole.
Habitat: Abundant on sand in depths greater than 50 feet.
Baits: Herring, clam parts, polycaetous worms.
Table value: Good.

Figure 47, Pacific Sanddab

Sandabs comprise an important segment of the flatfish catch. They are taken the year round. Average length is ten inches, with maximum length about 14 inches.

pacific salmon
spawning colors

With the onset of sexual maturity salmon lose their silvery ocean brightness and each species takes on its distinct spawning dress. The spawning colors of male salmon are brighter than those of the female, and the male also grows a hooked snout armed with large breeding teeth, a "razor" back and an enlarged adipose fin.

PINK SALMON
Female, top; male, bottom

CHINOOK SALMON
Male, top; female, bottom

CHUM SALMON
Male, top; female, bottom

COHO SALMON
Female, top; male, bottom

SOCKEYE SALMON
Male, top; female, bottom
(Jim Ames Photo)

SALMON!

Each of the five species of Pacific coast salmon are born in gravel beds in fresh water streams 10 to 700 miles from the sea. The various species, Chinook, silver, pink, sockeye and chum, do not spend equal lengths of time in fresh water or in the ocean, but all return to the river of their birth upon maturity.

The salmon stop feeding when entering fresh water, living on stored body fats. With tremendous power and desire they struggle upstream past falls, rapids, log jams and other obstructions until they reach the section of river where they were born. The female digs a redd or nest of about 18 inches depth and deposits up to 8,000 eggs. The male fertilizes the eggs by covering them with a milky substance known as milt. The fertilized eggs are covered with gravel and the salmon's life is finished. The fish drift downstream and die within a short period.

In the following pages color pictures tell the story from eyed salmon eggs to ocean-bound fingerlings.

EYED EGGS

About one month after the bright pink eggs have been deposited in the gravel, carefully covered against direct sunlight, the "eyes" start to show. Water flow and temperature is vital at this stage. Greatest mortality in the salmon's life cycle occurs in the eye-to-fry stage.

HATCHED ALEVINS

In about 60 days the eggs hatch and become alevins. They grow rapidly under the gravel for three to four months, drawing from the orange yolk sac which contain a complete and balanced diet. The vitelline vein, running through the centre of the sac, gains oxygen from the water. Fish are protected at this state, but good water flow is critical to survival.

NEWLY EMERGED FRY

In the spring the alevins lose their sacs and wiggle from the gravel as free-swimming fry of about one inch length. The fry feed on small insects and plankton and are in turn easy prey for larger fish.

FINGERLINGS

As seaward migrants of three to six inches the young salmon, now known as fingerlings, start their journey to the ocean. Their migration is usually keyed to a spring freshet. Studies have shown that high water at this vital time usually means good survival.

SALMON FISHIN'

... learn the rules and you'll boat fish!

Although five species of salmon range along the Northwest's coast, only three species provide action for sport salmon anglers. Chinook (kings) and silvers (coho) offer action every year, while the humpies (pinks) are available in odd-years.

The chinook and silvers show a preference for herring and other small fish, thus fishermen take them with much greater frequency than they do sockeye and chum salmon which feed on hard-shelled animals such as shrimp. The humpies switch from shrimp and similar food to herring during their second year of ocean life and are then taken in greater number by sports fishermen.

CHINOOK IS KING

King, chinook, tyee—by whatever name this heavy-shouldered salmon is called, he's among the top salt water

Chinook Salmon

Washington State Fisheries Dept.

fish found anywhere. Ranging in weight from 12 to 40 pounds, chinook usually are in their fourth year when they hit spawning riffles. Largest sport-caught chinook recorded is the 92 pounder taken from British Columbia's Skeena river in 1959 by Heinz Wichmann. Large as he was, the Skeena chinook was dwarfed by the trap-caught fish of 126 1/2 pounds which was taken years ago at Point Colpoys on Prince of Wales island, Alaska.

LEARN THE RULES

Those sport fishermen who consistently silver the floorboards in their boats with chinook salmon scales have spent time studying this trophy fish. They have learned the four "do's" of successful chinook angling:

1. Fish close to shore.
2. Fish slow.
3. Fish deep.
4. Fish early.

Like any other set of fishing rules, this group of "do's" is not absolute. They will vary from time to time, but nevertheless form the solid basis of hook-and-lining chinook salmon.

Chinook lead along shorelines on migration routes. They favor relatively shallow shelves that abruptly drop off into deep water. Points of land that project far out are naturals for the big fish since tides and currents at these locations create eddies and rips that gather bait fish.

Fishermen should avail themselves of the best marine chart for the area they want to fish and locate the sharp shallow/deep changes in water depth.

HERRING MOST EFFECTIVE

Slow moving baits and lures are most effective for chinook. Herring accounts for far more of these fish than plugs or spoons in salt water. Whole herring, plugged herring or slabs cut from large herring all tempt chinook, with hooks set so that the bait makes a slow erratic roll as does a crippled live herring.

Although chinook are found near surface at dawn, mature fish don't frequent the top 30 feet of water as do silver salmon. Standard chinook technique calls for spilling of line until the sinker hits bottom, then reeling in a few feet of line to hopefully move the bait out of striking-range of a myriad of bottom fish and into the strike zone of a cruising chinook. At first crack of light the salmon usually stage a "bite" for varying lengths of time. During this period chinook may be making slashing runs through schools of herring or other bait fish. Then he wheels to leisurely pick up cripples. Fishermen who work through patches of bait with their herring hooked so that it makes the slow, distressed roll that chinook are looking for are in business.

BOATS A MUST

Salt water chinook fishing is a

boat show. Trolling with motor or oars is most common way to present bait, but some anglers anchor on the lip of a drop-off where they cast and slowly retrieve bait to give it action. If the tide is running strong, it is possible to "soak" the bait, leaving it to the moving water to activate bait, either while anchored or when drifting with the tide. When salmon are in a picky mood it is wise to troll at different speeds to add variety to action of bait or lure. A proven chinook-catching gimmick is to slack off on oars or to place motor in neutral occasionally. When the lead hits bottom the boat is put in forward motion again. Zig-zag trolling is effective, also, since turns permit bait to settle with a tantalizing flutter.

CHINOOK HIT LIGHT

It is not common for chinook to strike hard. Even the heavy weights will often lightly mouth a bait before turning. Some experienced hands drop tip of their rod or feed 5 to 10 feet of line to the fish at the first gentle nudge. When the fish exerts a strong pull the hook is set. Characteristically a chinook will make one or more sizzling, flat runs when the hooks are jammed home. He then is prone to sound for a sulking spell on the bottom with little movement, before coming back near the surface under pressure of the rod.

SILVERS ROAM

Silver or coho salmon are classified as pelagic fish, that is "of the ocean surface ... of the open sea." Unlike chinook, they are not necessarily associated with a land mass and often are found in schools off shore. Tests have indicated that most silvers are cuaght, both by commercial and sport fishermen, in the top 30 feet of water. Two ounces of lead and 40 feet of line is usually sufficient to reach them.

WATCH FOR SIGNS

Since fishermen often have to roam to locate silvers, they must watch for the signs that say "fish." Wheeling and diving sea gulls usually denote concentrations of bait. By following a debris line which marks a current thread fishermen will sooner or later find a point where one or more other rips join. This action gathers bait fish and concentrates silvers under them.

Silvers aren't fussy about hitting hours. They may be taken through the day, but best periods occur around tide changes when more eddies are formed with resulting concentration of feed.

Silver Salmon

Washington State Fisheries Dept.

Most silvers taken by sports gear are between 6 and 14 pounds. Record for rod and line is 31 pounds. It was taken from Cowichan Bay on Vancouver Island, British Columbia, in 1947. In some areas of late run silvers these fish average 10 to 15 pounds with an occasional 20 pounder showing. Majority of silvers enter spawning streams from September to December.

Silvers spend up to one year in the stream of their birth, then head for the saltchuck early in their second year. Initially their diet is heavy on shrimp, but then they switch to herring and needlefish. They show prodigious growth during their third year, right up to the time they enter spawning streams.

FLIES ARE EFFECTIVE

Because silvers are surface cruisers, streamer flies are highly effective. When the silvery fish are stuffing themselves with every fish that wiggles past their zone of vision they will hit flies with abandon. There is no question when a silver grabs. The strike is sudden and hard, and almost invariably in followed by a line-consuming run punctuated with twisting leaps. Silvers lack the heft and staying power of chinook, but they must surely rank among the world's greatest game fish when taken on light tackle.

FISH 'EM FAST

While chinook prefer slow baits, the preference of silvers is fast spinning baits, darting flies or spoons presented in quick time. Streamer, or coho flies are trolled within sight of the boat so fast and near the surface that the wake of the fly may be readily seen.

Both chinook and silvers may be caught at mouths of rivers where they gang waiting for the surge of fresh water which sends them upstream to spawning beds. The salmon are more temperamental as they approach spawning time and are not so interested in herring, or other natural baits. Wobbling spoons or salmon plugs will catch more fish when the salmon are holding in brackish water off river mouths. Striking periods are apt to be shorter during this time. It is probably that the salmon have stopped feeding and hit lures out of irritation. While bright, clean salmon may be taken at river mouths, the chinook, particularly, start to darken. Most sportsmen prefer to meet the fish in the open sea.

USE HUSKY GEAR

Standard chinook salmon gear includes an 8 to 10 foot glass rod with a revolving spool reel capable of holding about 200 yards or more of 12 to 20 pound test line. Since chinook have hard mouths, a rod with a lot of starch in the butt section is best so that hooks can be rammed home past the barbs. Silver gear is similar, although a bit lighter. If dodgers or flashers are used (see diagrams) a shorter, stiffer rod should be selected as the drag is greater and more lead is needed to hold the dodger at desired level.

Sportiest terminal gear for both chinook and silvers consists of a kidney-type sinker of 2 to 4 ounces with a bead swivel attached to each end. Approximately 6 feet of 8 to 12 pound test leader is used. Either 1 or 2 hooks of 2/0, 3/0 or 4/0 size, depending upon size of bait, are common. Silver flies are trolled with no weight, or with 1 or 2 ounce sinkers.

—S.N.J.—

... this is what it's

all about!!

fishing methods, gear & bait

'bottomfish'

Northwest salt-water anglers categorize most fish they catch that are neither salmon nor trout as "bottomfish". When angling for these or any fish, the terminal gear (from the sinker to the hook) should vary with the habitat as well as the kind of fish sought. To fish the surf along sandy ocean beaches requires a rod and reel capable of casting a three ounce sinker a hundred feet or so. The sinker should be designed to hold in the surf and sand and rigged to allow the line to slip freely through a swivel eye so as not to discourage delicately biting surfperch (Figure 1). Pile perch and striped seaperch angling from piers or boats in the Northwest requires a different approach. These are wary fish and since the bait is often held off bottom, a light slip sinker is desirable. (Figure 5).

When boat fishing, the gear shown in Figure 4 is good for flatfish. If a herring bait is used, standard mooching rig is hard to beat and may also produce an incidental salmon. Live fish for bait is both effective and legal in our marine waters and requires a special approach. The hook-up pictured in Figure 3 is recommended for lingcod or large rockfish.

saltwater hookups

Figure 1

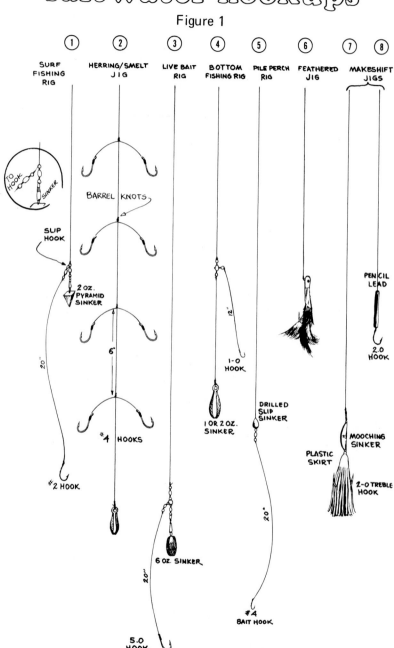

① SURF FISHING RIG
② HERRING/SMELT JIG
③ LIVE BAIT RIG
④ BOTTOM FISHING RIG
⑤ PILE PERCH RIG
⑥ FEATHERED JIG
⑦ ⑧ MAKESHIFT JIGS

TO HOOK / SINKER

SLIP HOOK

2 OZ. PYRAMID SINKER

BARREL KNOTS

20"

#2 HOOK

6'

#4 HOOKS

12'

1-0 HOOK

1 OR 2 OZ. SINKER

DRILLED SLIP SINKER

20"

#4 BAIT HOOK

20"

6 OZ. SINKER

20"

5-0 HOOK

PENCIL LEAD

2-0 HOOK

MOOCHING SINKER

PLASTIC SKIRT

2-0 TREBLE HOOK

early gear

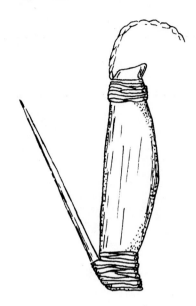

Nootka-type hook used for offshore salmon trolling

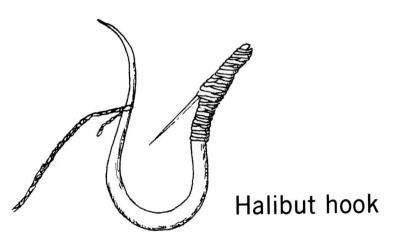

Halibut hook

natural baits Figure 9

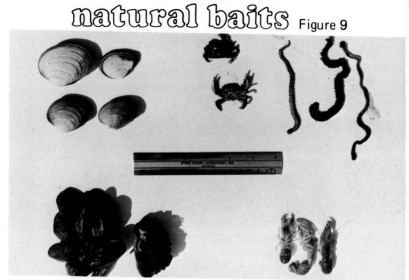

Figure 9. Easy to gather baits. From left to right (above): hardshell clams, shore crabs, polychaetous (pile, sand, etc.) worms, (below) mussels, ghost shrimp.

When fishing from rocks or jetties for rockfish, greenling, and lingcod, jigs (Figure 6) are often best because they can be fished away from "tackle grabbing" rocks and kelp. They are usually cast into a likely spot, allowed to sink, and worked in with a jerking motion of the rod tip. When boat fishing in deep water, jigs are not retrieved, but are simply jerked up and down just above the bottom. The plain lead jig is very effective as shown or it can be baited with a strip of fish belly, fish skin, or pork rind. Plain lead is attractive to fish and it is not unusual to see a rockfish, greenling, or even a salmon pass a bait to strike a sinker.

A variety of natural baits (Figure 9) are easily available to salt water anglers. Mussels can be picked from pilings or rocks when the tide is only moderately out. Even during the highest tide, they may be gathered from the submerged edges of moorage floats or buoys. Mussels are simply broken open and the soft flesh strung onto the hook. Parts of clams or cockles, especially the tough neck portions, are good baits for some kinds of fish. Razor clam necks stay on the hook well during the vigorous cast necessary for ocean surf fishing, and are often sold near the more popular ocean beaches.

Polycaetous worms (pile worms, sand worms, etc.) are superior bait. These worms can be found at moderately low tides by turning over rocks, digging in the sand, or from beneath barnacles and mussels broken from rocks or piles. Some lower tidal species construct long tube-shaped shells and will be found attached to the bottom or the submerged portions of floating docks. Many of these worms are predaceous and are capable of inflicting a pinching bite comparable to that of a large ant. Large worms can be divided into two or more baits.

Any of the shrimp and shrimp-like crustaceans are good bait. Ghost shrimp concentrations can be located at moderately low tides by the softening effect their "U" shaped burrows have on sandy flats. Suddenly sinking to ankle depth in sand is often indication of an abundance of these animals. Ghost shrimp can be collected by digging or by "treading" which collapses the burrows and causes the ghost shrimp to emerge from the sand. At low tide, true shrimp can often be collected from tide pools or from beneath the fronds of kelp and other seaweeds. Shore crabs are another good bait and are very easy to collect from under rocks and debris at most tidal stages.

Herring, although not necessarily the best, is the most common of all local salt-water bait. Packaged frozen herring is available at most establishments catering to salt-water fishermen and some boathouses sell live bait. Frequently fishermen will encounter herring while fishing and if prepared, can collect them on the spot. During late fall through early spring on Puget Sound and Juan de Fuca Strait, certain diving birds, especially the rhinoceros auklet, will cause a school of herring to compact into a spherical mass near the surface. Gulls are quick to locate these "herring balls" and will gather in a tight group above the bait and repeatedly dive into the massed fish. If an angler has sewn a piece of small mesh net (as is used for smelt dipping) into the bottom of his landing net, has learned to recognize the gulls' behavior, and is quick to react, he may have to use restraint not to dip more bait than he can use. More often herring can be collected by "jigging". The jig (Figure 2) is lowered into a school of herring and jerked every few seconds. Herring are attracted to the shiny hooks and either strike or are snagged.

Herring and some other fishes are very good live bait for large rockfish and lingcod. Live greenling, small rockfish, and flounders are excellent bait for large lingcod. Many local fishermen have taken their largest lingcod accidentally when one of these fierce fish has attacked another fish they were trying to land. Frequently, under these circumstances, the lingcod will not even be hooked but will simply be grasping the impromptu "bait" in its mouth — the bait may even be another lingcod!

Herring and other fishes can be kept alive in a large container, such as a plastic garbage can, if not overcrowded and if fresh seawater is frequently added. Live bait fish should be hooked rather lightly in the flesh beneath the dorsal fin or above the anal fin.

SPORT SALMON TERMINAL GEAR

MOOCHING GEAR

5 TO 6' NYLON   CUT PLUG

HERRING BAITS
CUT SPINNER
WHOLE HERRING

MOOCHING GEAR. This type of equipment is a favorite of fishermen looking for maximum sport. Sinkers of one to six ounces are used. Herring is activated by trolling, wind or tide action, or by reeling or stripping line in.

COHO FLY

1/2 ACTUAL SIZE

COHO FLY. These colorful flies are killers for coho when trolled fast near the surface with little or no lead. Polar bear hair is usually used for hackle. Coho flies fished deep behind dodgers or flashers will take kings.

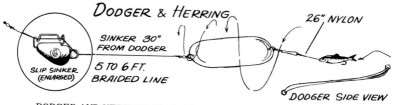

DODGER & HERRING

26" NYLON

SINKER 30"
FROM DODGER

SLIP SINKER
(ENLARGED)

5 TO 6 FT.
BRAIDED LINE

DODGER SIDE VIEW

DODGER AND HERRING. The bright, erratic flash of the dodger attracts both kings and silvers, while the herring offers food appeal. Spoons or coho flies are often successfully substituted for herring.

STANDARD LARGE SPOON OR PLUG GEAR

18 TO 20' BRAIDED LINE   6' WIRE   LOOP DIAMETER OF PENCIL

SPOON SIDE VIEW

STANDARD LARGE SPOON OR PLUG GEAR. Maturing kings found at river mouths are attracted by this gear. Advantages are that fish other than salmon are not so likely to hit, and that plugs and spoons are working all the time.

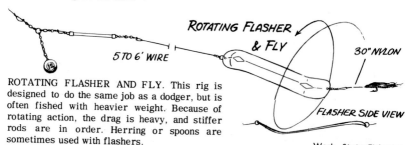

ROTATING FLASHER & FLY

30" NYLON

5 TO 6' WIRE

FLASHER SIDE VIEW

ROTATING FLASHER AND FLY. This rig is designed to do the same job as a dodger, but is often fished with heavier weight. Because of rotating action, the drag is heavy, and stiffer rods are in order. Herring or spoons are sometimes used with flashers.

Wash. State Fisheries

salmon hook knots

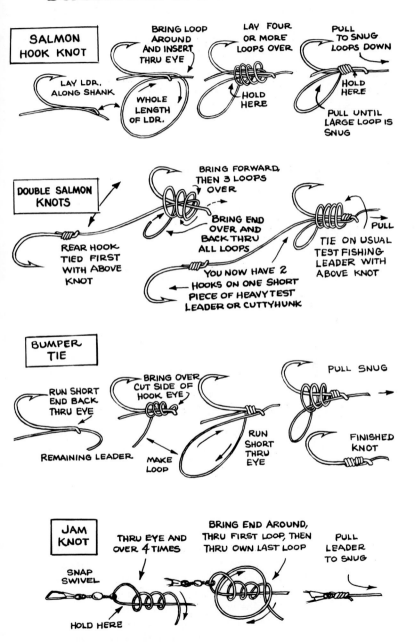

SALMON HOOK KNOT

LAY LDR. ALONG SHANK

BRING LOOP AROUND AND INSERT THRU EYE

WHOLE LENGTH OF LDR.

LAY FOUR OR MORE LOOPS OVER

HOLD HERE

PULL TO SNUG LOOPS DOWN

HOLD HERE

PULL UNTIL LARGE LOOP IS SNUG

DOUBLE SALMON KNOTS

REAR HOOK TIED FIRST WITH ABOVE KNOT

BRING FORWARD, THEN 3 LOOPS OVER

BRING END OVER AND BACK THRU ALL LOOPS

YOU NOW HAVE 2 HOOKS ON ONE SHORT PIECE OF HEAVY TEST LEADER OR CUTTYHUNK

PULL

TIE ON USUAL TEST FISHING LEADER WITH ABOVE KNOT

BUMPER TIE

RUN SHORT END BACK THRU EYE

REMAINING LEADER

BRING OVER CUT SIDE OF HOOK EYE

MAKE LOOP

RUN SHORT THRU EYE

PULL SNUG

FINISHED KNOT

JAM KNOT

SNAP SWIVEL

HOLD HERE

THRU EYE AND OVER 4 TIMES

BRING END AROUND, THRU FIRST LOOP, THEN THRU OWN LAST LOOP

PULL LEADER TO SNUG

mooching salmon

Mooching is currently the most popular salmon angling technique in the Northwest. It is popular because it is effective, involves relatively light simple gear, and it is conducive to groups of people fishing from one boat such as those used for chartering. Mooching terminal gear (Figure 10) consists of a special 1 to 5 ounce banana-shaped sinker usually equipped with swivels at both ends, a 7 foot leader and a bait fish, cut or whole, rigged so that it spins when moved slowly through the water. Monofilament nylon line and leader is used, and most often tests between 8 and 20 pounds breaking strength. Mooching rods range from 7½ to 9½ feet long, have a light action and cork handles consisting of a long butt end, fixed reel seat and short forepiece. Mooching reels are usually light salt water rotating spool models.

Hooks used for mooching range from sizes 1/0 to 4/0 depending upon the length of the 4 to 8 inch bait. Two hooks tied closely together in tandem are most commonly used, with the trailing hook a size smaller. Some anglers, however, think that a single hook is easier to bait, quicker to replace (important when dogfish are abundant), and equally as efficient for hooking chinook if the fish is given time to take the bait. In addition, sub-legal salmon caught with a single hook are easily released.

Mooching requires bait movement which is often attained by the actions of current, wind, and waves on a drifting boat. When fishing from either a drifting or propelled boat, the line angle into the water should be 40 to 60 degrees (Figure 11) for chinook. A "flatter" angle of 20 to 40 degrees is better for coho. (Figure 12). These angles are caused by the difference between the movements of the boat and the water and it is often necessary to use motor (or oars) to attain the proper line angle. This is more frequently the case with coho which are usually within 30 feet of the surface. The mark of an inexperienced angler is too "flat" a line angle (caused by excessive speed) and too much line out resulting in the angler not knowing his fishing depth.

Chinook are found at various depths, but are frequently just off bottom. Mooching gear is effective for chinook because it can easily be fished at a variety of depths and it is very effective while sinking or being retrieved. In deeper water, many chinook take the bait when it is sinking, causing the bite to feel as though the lead has prematurely hit bottom. Often, when wind or tides are too strong, the motor should be used negatively — that is to lessen the natural drift to increase the line angle. When running the motor at a slow trolling speed, shifting in and out of gear, reversing, or changing direction (all causing the bait to fish vertically) are very effective. This is especially true in water deeper than 50 feet. A good moocher fishes the bait vertically as well as horizontally and frequently uses his motor or oars to adjust line angle.

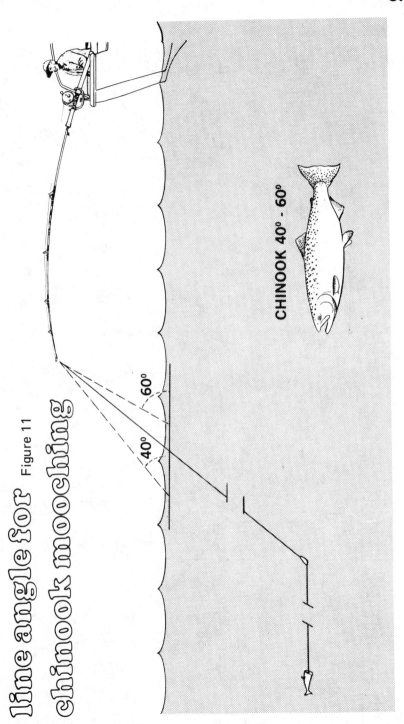

line angle for chinook mooching

Figure 11

CHINOOK 40° - 60°

60°

40°

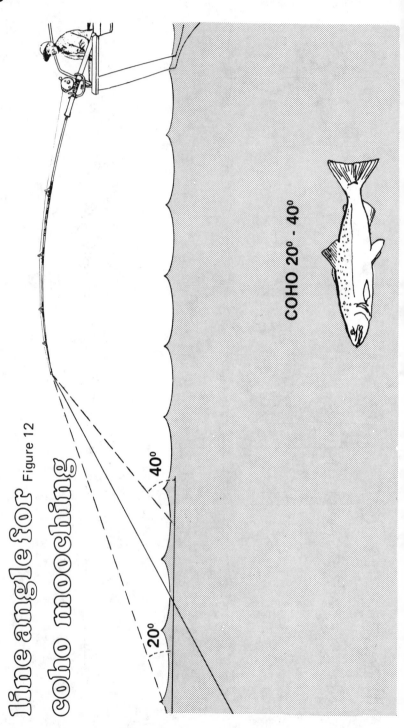

line angle for Figure 12
coho mooching

40°

20°

COHO 20° - 40°

A typical chinook bite on mooching gear is only a nibble. Usually chinook quickly bite a bait fish once or twice, often spit it out between bites, and then finally take it deeply. At the first nibble, experienced anglers recommend the following:

Immediately "feed" the fish a few yards of slack line, wait until the fish appears to move off steadily and then set the hook by quickly tightening the line (not jerking). Often, when using this method, the fish will move toward the boat and a considerable length of line must be retrieved before the line comes tight. Many chinook are not hooked because the bait is pulled away from them before they take it deeply.

When using a rod holder, the reel should be adjusted so that any tension, in addition to the drag through the water, will take line from the reel. Often the reel "click" alone will serve this purpose. When holding the rod, a thumb can be used to control the line tension. A simple reel and a trained thumb make a good combination.

For coho, the usually faster moving bait and a different feeding behavior results in a more spectacular bite that can properly be termed a "strike". Coho are often hooked when they first take the bait. When using a rod holder, the drag is usually adjusted tight enough to set the hook. For this reason, a two hook mooching rig may be best for coho fishing. However, many are hooked with a single hook mooching rig using the same "feeding" method previously described for chinook. When coho are only "pecking" at one's bait (as they often do), this technique may even be more productive.

How to identify Chinook Salmon

Most COHO have only a few spots on upper tail. CHINOOK salmon have many spots on upper and lower tail.

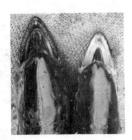

CHINOOK always have black lower gum line. COHO always have white lower gum line.

herring cutting and hooking

There is nothing mystical or difficult about putting a good herring bait on a hook. The following illustrations cover methods for baiting a whole herring, a plug cut, and a cut spinner. For the cut baits, you need a sharp knife for clean cuts to give the finished bait the proper action. Freshly killed herring for whole or plug cut baits are preferred, but the cut spinner can only properly be made from frozen herring. As a general rule, the best frozen or fresh bait is thin ("starved out") because it is firm and is more inclined to stay on the hook. Avoid packaged frozen bait that is discolored or ragged in appearance. Pack fresh herring in ice so that it stays out of the water formed as the ice melts and it lays straight. Herring, thus cared for, remains firm for about 30 hours.

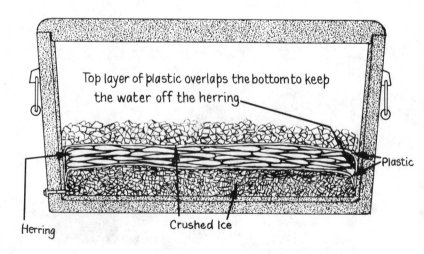

Top layer of plastic overlaps the bottom to keep the water off the herring.

Plastic

Herring

Crushed Ice

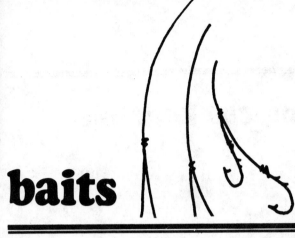

baits

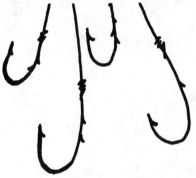

RECOMMENDED HOOK SIZES

Double hooks are used in the following illustrations, but if a single hook is preferred, the same procedure is followed except the trailing hook is absent. The following hook sizes are recommended for the bait size indicated:

Length (inches) finished bait	Double hook sizes Lead Hook	Trailing Hook	Single Hook Sizes
3 1/2 — 4 1/2	1/0	1	1/0
4 1/2 — 5 1/2	2/0	1/0	2/0
5 1/2 — 6 1/2	3/0	2/0	3/0
6 1/2 — 7 1/2	4/0	3/0	4/0

The herring baits described are supposed to spin. Before lowering the bait to fishing depth, it should first be tested by pulling it through the water while in view alongside the boat.

plug-cut herring

Top left, trailing hook. Top center, lead hook.

A sharp knife and a herring are the basic ingredients for plug-cut herring fishing. This is a highly popular salmon bait and is very easy to cut and rig. Plug-sized herring are from five to seven inches long before they are beheaded.

1. Lay the herring on a board and cut the head off, in back of the pectoral fins, at about a 45 degree angle.

2. Remove the entrails by trapping them against the cutting board with the knife point and pulling the plugged bait away.

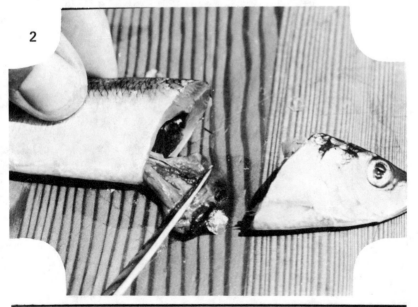

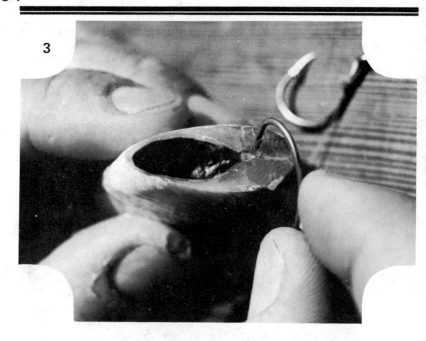

3/4. Insert the point of the trailing hook into the face of the cut so that the hook passes through the spine and out the side of the bait. Pull the hook and leader clear through the herring and follow through with the other hook.

5/6. Seat the trailing hook in the side of the herring that is opposite the side from which the leader emerges.

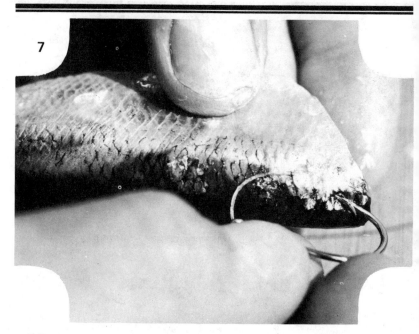

7/8. Seat the lead hook in the other side of the bait. The hook point should enter just in front of where the leader emerges from the skin. Pull the leader gently so as to completely seat the lead hook and the bait is ready to test.

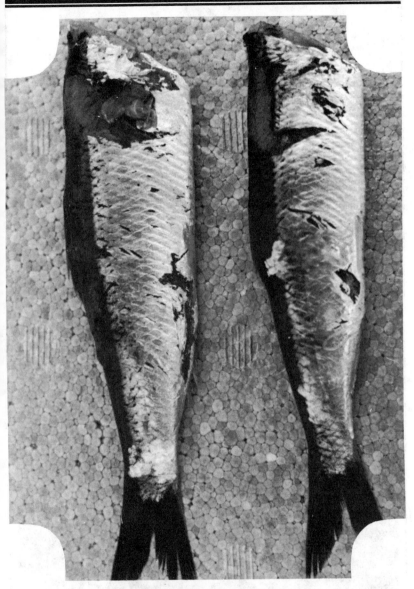

SALMON TEETH MARKS

Teeth marks like these mean salmon! The left plug-cut herring was taken by a 10-12 pound chinook and the right bait by a coho of about 15 inches. In both cases, the salmon were observed. The larger fish left well-spaced, deep puncture wounds whereas the small coho tended to scrape the bait. The large open wounds in the front portions of the herring were inflicted by the hooks being pulled free.

This white sturgeon picked up a herring bait in Puget Sound at Duwamish Head, proving that herring will take most any species of fish. It weighed 25 pounds. (F&H News' Photo)

whole herring

Whole herring are preferred when bait is too small, (less than 5" long) or it is too soft to plug cut. A soft whole herring stays on a hook better than a soft plugged herring. Occasionally, for big chinook, large, whole herring are effective.

1/2. Insert the trailing hook's point into the "silt" under the lower jaw and pull the hook and leader up through the herring's snout. Follow through with the lead hook.

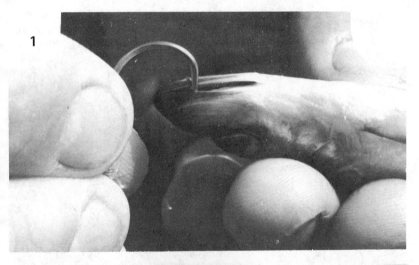

1

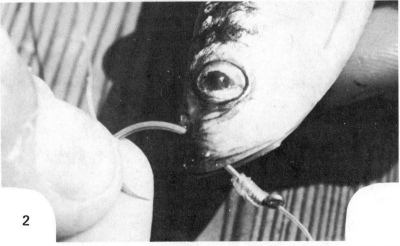

2

3. Insert the trailing hook's point into the upper edge of the eye socket, without damaging the eye itself, and bring the hook point out the corresponding spot on the other side. Pull the hook clear through and follow' with the lead hook.

4/5. Seat the trailing hook in the side of the herring that is opposite the side from which the leader emerges from the eye socket.

6. Seat the lead hook in the other side of the bait, near the head.

7. Gently pull the leader in front of herring to take up the slack, and the bait is ready to test.

cut spinners

CUT SPINNERS. Two of these baits are cut from each large (9-11 inch) herring. Consistent spinner cutting requires a razor-sharp knife (especially near the point) and a herring that is frozen stiff. For this reason, spinners are usually cut just before leaving shore or cut and re- frozen for longer periods of time. Unlike the plug cut and whole herring baits, spinner cutting does require a little practice and finesse.

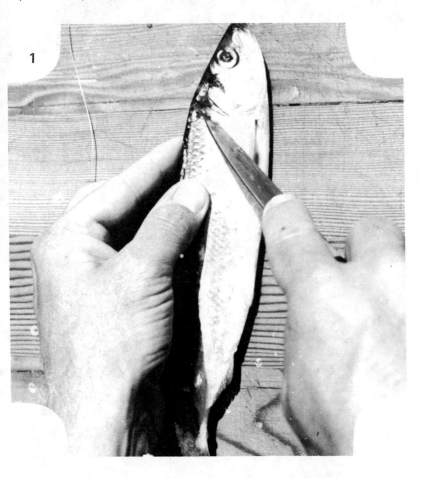

1/2/3. Make a straight cut, beveled at about 45 degrees, behind the gill covers. Do not cut deeper than the middle of the herring. Make the second and third cuts shallow above the belly and below the back.

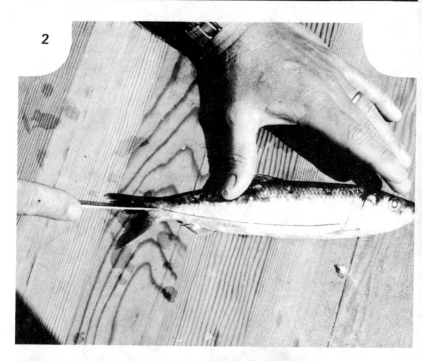

2

3

4

4/5. Holding the herring against the cutting board, insert the knife alongside the dorsal fin so that the knife's flat side is against the spine, and push the blade through the belly cut. Work the blade forward, while holding it flat against the spine, until it passes through the first cut.

5

6. Turn the knife so that the cutting edge is toward the tail, re-insert the blade into the same cut and work it toward the tail, holding the blade flat against the spine. Remove the spinner and scrape away any entrails adhering to the body cavity wall.

6

7

7/8. The spinner should look something like this.

8

9. Insert the trailing hook into the flesh side of the spinner and pull the hook out the scale side. Follow through the same hole with the lead hook.

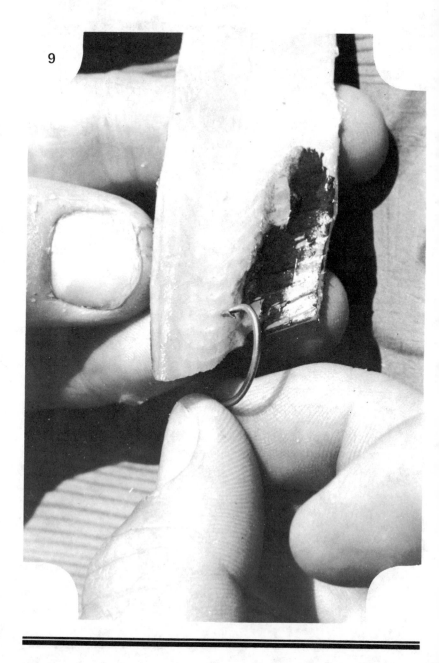
9

10

10/11. Seat the lead hook into the scaled side of the bait. The hook point should enter the skin just in front of the hole where the leader emerges from the scales. Let the trailing hook hang free, and the spinner is ready to test.

11

live herring

Nothing looks more like a live, injured herring than the genuine article. Live bait is used to good advantage by many Canadian anglers, but by only a few knowledgeable U.S. fishermen. Ronald B. Stokes of Vancouver, British Columbia, has given advice on live baiting with herring. Obviously, of primary importance to successful live bait fishing is keeping the bait alive. The critical factors are: (1) a suitable container; (2) cool, clean seawater; and (3) adequate dissolved oxygen in the water.

A plastic garbage can, of 20-gallon capacity, makes an acceptable container. Galvanized metal is toxic to fish, as are some plastic containers treated with substances to kill bacteria. A plastic bag type liner should be used if you are not sure if the container has been so treated. The container should only be about half filled with water to prevent spillage.

Water temperature is important when air temperatures exceed 60 degrees F. Herring require more oxygen and space with higher temperatures. The water can be cooled by replacing it with fresh seawater or with ice sealed in a plastic bag.

Like most other fishes, herring must take dissolved oxygen from the water. In order to keep herring healthy in a small container, the water must be frequently aerated. This can be done by dipping water from the bait container, with a smaller pail, and pouring it back from a 2 or 3-foot height. A simple aeration pump can be fashioned from a hand or air mattress pump, by attaching a length of aquarium or surgical tubing between the pump and an aquarium aeration stone. Aeration stones, available at most pet stores, break the air into small bubbles which allow the oxygen to be more readily absorbed into the water.

Experienced live baiters prefer small, sharp hooks. A No. 6 single lead hook with a No. 6 treble hook trailing is a favorite with Canadian experts. The lead hook is inserted near the nostrils with the treble hooked lightly in back of the dorsal fin.

Live Herring Hook-up

Small front hook through nostrils

back hook just under skin behind fin

A light mooching lead, weighing about 1 1/2 ounces, and a 6-foot leader and a light mooching rod are recommended. Since the live herring provides its own action, it is usually fished from a drifting or anchored boat. When fishing over depths exceeding 50 feet, the usual method is to drop the bait to the bottom and then quickly raise it about 25 feet where it is fished. At dawn or just before dark, it is usually advantageous to fish the bait within 25 feet of the surface.

A typical salmon take of a live herring transmits only a light tap followed by a slack line as the fish moves toward the surface. At other times, the salmon will move laterally with the bait and anglers must be prepared to let line run free. No matter how the bait is taken, the salmon must be given the opportunity to take the bait deeply before setting the hook. Because of the salmon's habit of moving toward the surface after taking the bait, it may be necessary to retrieve most of the line before it becomes tight to the fish.

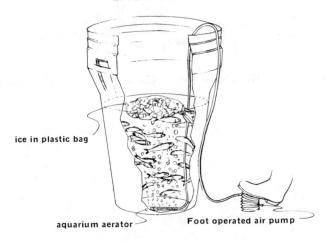

Live Bait Container

ice in plastic bag

aquarium aerator

Foot operated air pump

trolling

Some of the popular trolling gear is illustrated in Figure 10. Salmon are usually hooked as soon as they strike trolling lures. The strike is typically spectacular when compared to a bite on mooching gear. A variety of lines, rods and reels are suitable for trolling, depending largely upon the drag of the lures, type of line, and the length of the terminal gear. The trolling rod tip should be sensitive enough to reveal the action of the gear. Proper trolling speeds vary with the gear being used. If one is unfamiliar with a particular piece of terminal trolling gear, it pays to adhere to the manufacturer's recommendations.

rotating flasher fishing

The authors recently undertook a program that involved catching, tagging, and releasing hundreds of chinook and coho salmon in the Seattle-Tacoma area of Puget Sound. The program had several objectives but one was to get some idea of how many salmon were available to efficient anglers. In order to do this, rotating flasher gear was used because it is considered to be the most effective sport gear available.

In 43 days of fishing, using four rods and one boat, a total of 1,100 chinook and coho salmon were caught in various locations between Fox Island and Point No Point. This catch included only two or three dogfish sharks and a dozen or so other fishes. This program indicates that the average Puget Sound angler, who currently averages between 0.1 and 0.2 salmon per day, could increase his catch by a factor of 10 by using flasher gear. Those anglers about to give up on salmon because of a lack of success, should first try the methods outlined below. If, after a decent attempt, they are still unsuccessful, perhaps trying another sport is in order.

Rotating flashers are designed to turn over in the water. This action produces an attracting flash, resembling the silvery sides of a hungry salmon attacking a school of bait, and it gives the trailing lure a darting action. "Dodgers" are used in a similar manner, but they are trolled at a slower speed and are designed to "wobble" rather than to rotate (however, when trolled too fast, Dodgers will rotate). A proper rod, reel, line and rod holder are all essential for effective flasher fishing.

the rod

THE ROD — A suitable flasher rod has high quality hard guides, a sturdy reel seat and handle, and is about nine feet long. In addition, it has sufficient backbone to handle a flasher and 20 ounces of lead and yet a tip sensitive enough to dip with the action of the flasher. A long rod is needed to cope with the length of gear between sinker and hook. Attempting to net or gaff a fish using a rod shorter than one's terminal gear is a scene that often evokes the remark:

"He should have brought along a step ladder".

The nine foot Betts rod No. 5318 comes close to meeting these standards and was used in the tagging study previously mentioned. There are, however, other suitable rods on the market.

rotating flasher Figure 13

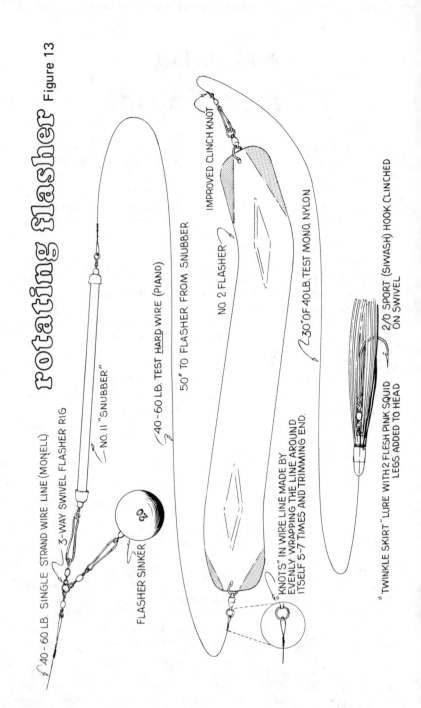

40 - 60 LB. SINGLE STRAND WIRE LINE (MONELL)

3-WAY SWIVEL FLASHER RIG

NO. II "SNUBBER"

FLASHER SINKER

40 - 60 LB. TEST HARD WIRE (PIANO)

50" TO FLASHER FROM SNUBBER

IMPROVED CLINCH KNOT

NO. 2 FLASHER

"KNOTS" IN WIRE LINE MADE BY EVENLY WRAPPING THE LINE AROUND ITSELF 5-7 TIMES AND TRIMMING END.

30" OF 40 LB. TEST MONO. NYLON

"TWINKLE SKIRT" LURE WITH 2 FLESH PINK SQUID LEGS ADDED TO HEAD

2/0 SPORT (SIWASH) HOOK CLINCHED ON SWIVEL

the line

THE LINE - Consistently effective flasher fishing is metal line fishing. Nylon lines are only satisfactory when salmon are uncommonly close to the surface. Not only is it difficult to reach a significant depth with nylon and flasher, but its stretch distorts the "message" of flasher action. Preferred line is single strand Monel of about 50 pounds breaking strength. With a little getting used to, metal line fishing offers no particular problem although kinks must be avoided because they will result in a broken line. Some care must be taken to wind line evenly, and under tension, onto the spool.

the reel

THE REEL — Use of single strand metal line requires a husky, large spooled reel such as the Pflueger Pakron. The Penn 49 is also a favorite among those using braided metal lines as well as single strand Monel (few other reels are suitable for metal line fishing).

the rod holder

THE ROD HOLDER — A sturdy, adjustable rod holder is almost essential for flasher fishermen. The Minzer meets the requirements. The drag of the flasher and lead through the water makes holding the rod uncomfortable for any length of time and if the reel drag is properly set, hand holding the rod is of no advantage. In addition, if more than one person is fishing from a boat, rod holders help keep the lines apart. Flashers are efficient line braiders when fished too close together.

trolling speed

TROLLING SPEED — Flashers are trolled faster than almost any other salmon gear. For this reason they are well adapted to boats that cannot maintain slower trolling speeds. Generally, they should be trolled just fast enough to produce a uniform rotation that transmits a smooth "beat" to the rod tip. The tip dips when the flasher swings low in its arc and raises when it is high. A flasher trolled too rapidly will also rotate and produce rhythmic rod action, but one trolled too slowly or fouled with drift will transmit jerky tip action. One should occasionally check for excessive speed by slowing down to make sure he is just above the threshold speed for uniform rotation. A constant motor speed is not the answer to effective trolling because of changing winds and currents.

trolling depth

TROLLING DEPTH — One of the standard questions asked by inexperienced anglers, inquiring about the details of a good catch, is:

"How much lead were you using?"

This inevitable query is meaningless. Fishing depth depends on line material and diameter, length of line fished, trolling speed, currents, wind, terminal gear as well as sinker weight. The meaningful question is:

"How deep were you fishing?"

Good fishermen know how deep they are fishing and they know how to duplicate and vary fishing depth.

It pays to experiment with depth. For this reason, two good trollers in a boat are usually more effective, per individual, than a lone fisherman. Using the "team" approach, one angler can fish at the depth that is usually productive and the other can experiment above and below this level. When fish are located both sets of gear can be zeroed in on the productive depth. We have often used this technique to good advantage. A fisherman could calibrate his reel so that he can interpret revolutions into line length.

Because of the position of a salmon's eyes on its head and since the source of light in water is from above, salmon are probably more apt to rise to lures than descend to them. It appears, therefore, that a lure presented above salmon is better than having the lure the same distance below the fish. However, because of excessive speeds and poor tackle, the most common trolling mistake is fishing too shallow — especially when chinook are involved. Coho and pink salmon are "semi-consistently" within 30 feet of the surface. However, coho are frequently found most abundant at depths to 75 feet.

A flasher outfit fishing properly.

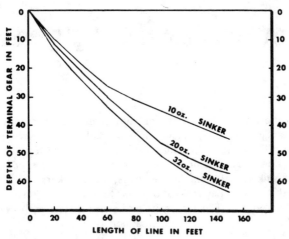

Approximate depths reached using rotating flasher gear (at "proper" trolling speed), from 0-150 feet of .028 inch solid Monel line, and 10, 20, and 32 oz. sinkers. Since a fishing line angle changes (flattens) with increasing line length, the graph lines do not reflect the path of a line through the water - only the approximate depth of the terminal gear using a specific length of line.

PRINCIPALS AND TIPS — Well equipped flasher fishermen will have leads of varying weights to fish properly under different conditions, especially to separate the gear effectively when using the "team" approach. Leads of 10, 16, 20, or 24, and 32 ounce weights will cover virtually all conditions.

For the beginner, a 20 ounce lead is a good all-around size.

The flasher should be let out carefully while the boat is underway and the revolutions of the reel counted so that depth can later be duplicated or varied. The rod should be placed in a rod holder set so that the rod, if not under stress, would be perpendicular to the gunnel and parallel with the water's surface. The drag is adjusted so that a pull, in addition to the drag of the gear, of about three pounds takes line from the reel. The reel click should be on when the gear is fishing, but off while reeling in and letting out line to keep it from wearing out.

Flasher fishing is often ridiculed by light tackle enthusiasts or those anxious to conceal their envy of a good catch. The frequent jibes at this time go something like this:

"With all that weight and other grabage, how do you know when you have a fish on?" or, "If you have to use all that junk to catch fish, I don't want any!"

The fact is that this equipment is so sensitive that an experienced angler can detect even a small piece of drift fouled on his terminal gear. A strike from even a small fish is very obvious and absolutely spectacular in contrast to the typical mooching bite. The sudden and frequent scream of the reel, the sight and feel of a thrashing rod and the absence of dogfish all tend to compensate for the clumsier aspects of flasher fishing. Also, many anglers overlook the use of flashers gear in conjunction with typical light mooching gear. Because flasher gear is trolled rapidly and can fish at all productive depths, it is excellent for exploring large areas in a short period of time. It is often productive in "zeroing in" on schools of fish in new areas, or familiar ones when the bite is slow.

other trolling gear

Fishing the proper depth has, for good reason, been emphasized in the previous paragraphs. Diving-plane sinkers are becoming very popular and provide an efficient means of maintaining considerable trolling depths with ordinary nylon lines. Cut or whole herring baits are most commonly used with these sinkers. Although some diving-plane sinkers can be used with flashers and dodgers, they make it difficult to read the action of the attractor through the rod tip. The strong pull of these sinkers is, however, all but eliminated when tripped by a hooked salmon.

DIVING-PLANE SINKER

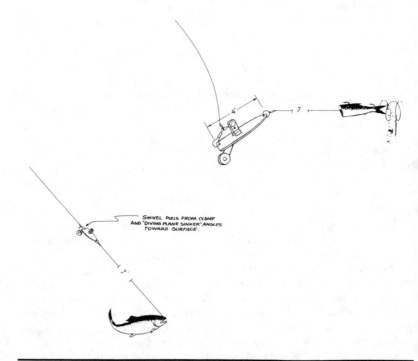

SWIVEL PULLS FROM CLAMP
AND "DIVING PLANE SINKER" ANGLES
TOWARD SURFACE.

jetty fishing

Popular salmon fisheries have developed off some jetties along the coast. Jetties on both the Oregon and Washington sides of the Columbia river are best. Other Oregon jetty spots include Garibaldi, Sandlake and Siletz, while the south jetty at Westport in Washington is popular. Salmon can be taken from these jetties by casting spoons, although herring fished with a float arrangement is the most popular (Figure 14). The float, sinker, and bait are cast out away from the jetty. The sinker then pulls the line down, through the float, to the depth governed by the "stopper knot"—usually placed 4 - 10 feet above the sinker. The float holds the bait, cut and hooked as for mooching (Figure 14), off the bottom where it spins in the channel current.

The jetty herring rig diagrammed is a modification of a rig commonly used. The float is an inexpensive 3" styrofoam ball, purchased from a variety store. A hole is punched through the center of the float with a long, straight instrument of small diameter (approximately 1/8").

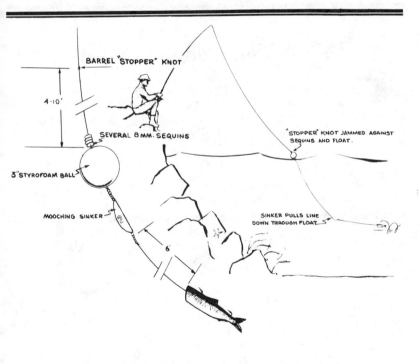

JETTY FISHING   Figure 14

filleting, skinning and steaking

by nick pasquale

The following series of illustrations and techniques have been designed to assist salt-water fishermen in preparing their catches of bottomfish for cooking. There is no need for the enjoyment to end when the boat is docked. Continued satisfaction from the fishing trip can be had by sitting down to a meal of really fresh fish. A good many anglers are somewhat awed by the shapes of the various species of bottom fish that they have caught and wonder:

Nick Pasquale

bottomfish, salmon

"Well, we got 'em, now what do we do with 'em?"

Actually, all one needs is patience, practice, and the proper fillet knife to make his catch ready for the skillet.

A typical catch will usually contain both flounders and roundfish, such as rockfish, lingcod, and Pacific cod. The basic filleting techniques will be nearly identical for all flatfish, as will the techniques for filleting roundfish. All bottomfish need not be filleted. Some may be filleted. Some may be dressed and cut into steaks, or some may be prepared to be utilized whole.

equipment

The equipment shown eases the task of preparing the catch for cooking and should include the following:

1. A SMOOTH PIECE OF ¾-INCH PLYWOOD about 15 inches by 36 inches. The size of the board can vary to suit individual needs. One side may be used for dressing and cutting up fish, reserving the smoothest side for filleting fish. A smooth, flat board is a must when cutting the skin from a fillet.

2. A FINE OIL STONE. Under normal use, a good oil stone should last nearly a lifetime. The original investment should be for the best stone available. A Washita stone is an excellent one. A light oil provides a good cutting medium and a dash of lighter fluid with the oil keeps the stone from getting gummy and also gives it more "cut".

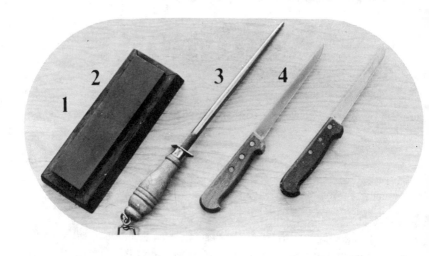

3. A STEEL. A steel is not a knife sharpener but a tool used to "set up" the edge on a knife that has been honed on a stone and should be used sparingly. A couple of light passes of the knife edge on the steel is usually sufficient to restore the cutting edge of the knife.

4. THE KNIVES. One good quality fillet knife and one stiff knife suitable for cutting through the backbone of some fishes are recommended. Here again, the knife should be the best available. For normal sportsman use, a knife should last indefinitely. Good quality, stainless steel knives are available at marine supply stores.

5. A COTTON GLOVE (LEFT HAND). A washable, cotton glove is a most necessary item. Not only does it allow the fish to be held securely but it also protects your hand from the numerous spines present on some truly edible fishes.

preparing flounder

filleting

The most common method of removing the edible portions of a good-size flounder is by filleting. This method yields two boneless fillets of excellent quality.

1. Remove the fillet from the white side first. Grasp the head in the left hand and make a shallow, diagonal cut from behind the head extending just past the mid-line of the fish. This allows the next cut to pass behind the stomach cavity.

1

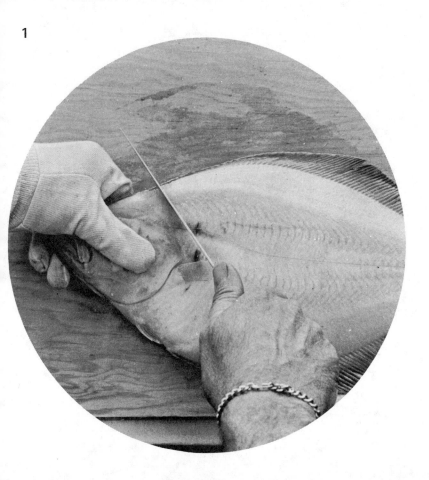

2/3/4. Turn the fish so the tail is nearly straight away from the working edge of the cutting board. The next cut is made with the knife inserted just to the right of the lateral line, a distinct series of scales showing as a line about midway from head to tail on the fish. With the knife held flat side up, insert the tip and make the thrust towards the tail, and at the same time cutting towards the edge of the fish. When making this cut, a slight downward pressure on the knife blade is necessary to keep the flat side of the knife gliding on the surface of the backbone.

2

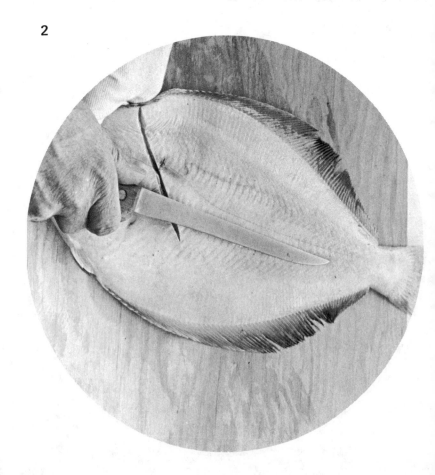

3

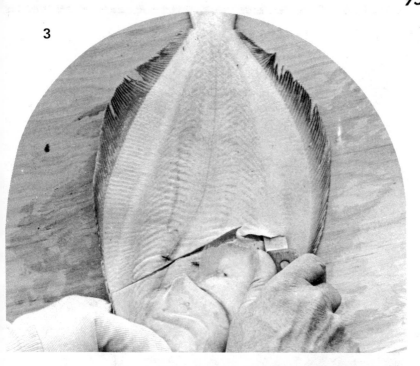

4

5/6. The third cut is made with the knife tip, starting from the tail end of the fillet. Hold up the cut part of the fillet and position the knife as shown (See 5). Exert enough downward pressure on the knife tip to make it bend and glide over the backbone, bring the cut forward to the head.

5

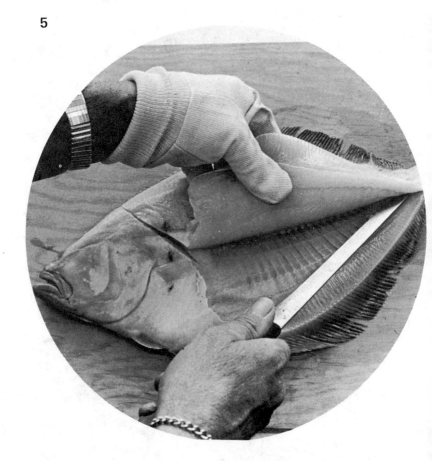

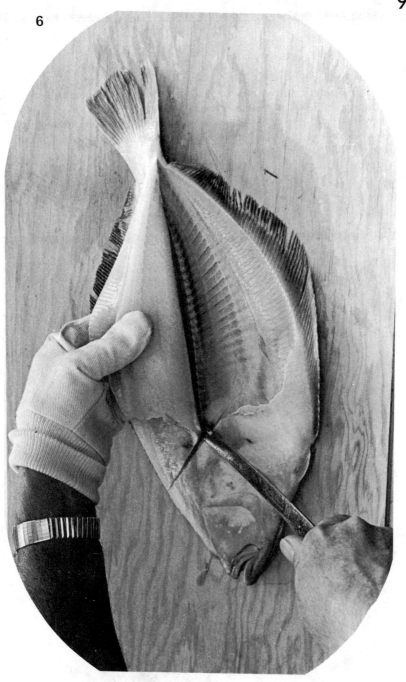

7/8/9. This cut removes the fillet from the fish. While holding up the cut portion of the fillet, start with the knife held flat in cut No. 1, cutting edge towards the tail. Exert a downward pressure to flex the knife blade to follow over the contour of the backbone, and cutting towards the tail, completely sever the fillet from the fish.

7

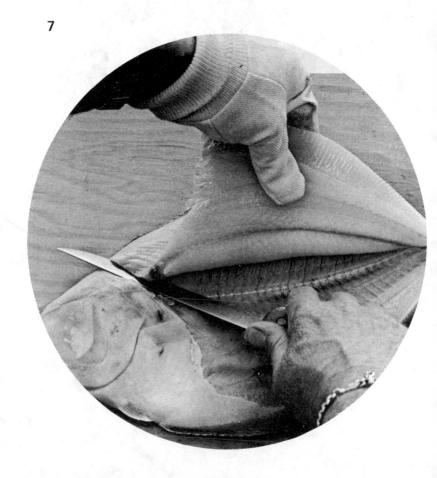

8

9

10/11/12. Now, turn the dark side of the fish up. The first cut on this side starts as a short, shallow, diagonal cut made in the thick, fleshy part directly in back of the head of the fish. Do not cut through the backbone. Next, insert the blade of the knife in this cut keeping the knife flat with cutting edge toward the tail. With a downward pressure on the blade to keep the flat side of the knife blade gliding over the backbone, cut to the end of the tail. Gauge the position of the knife tip so it will be following down the midline of the fish.

10

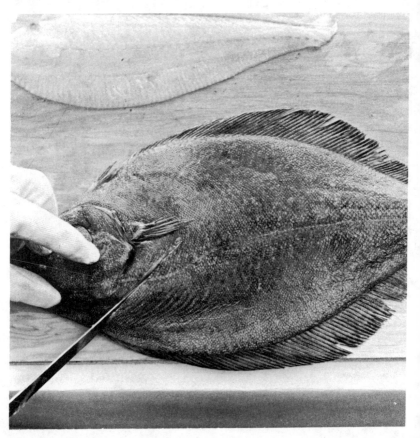

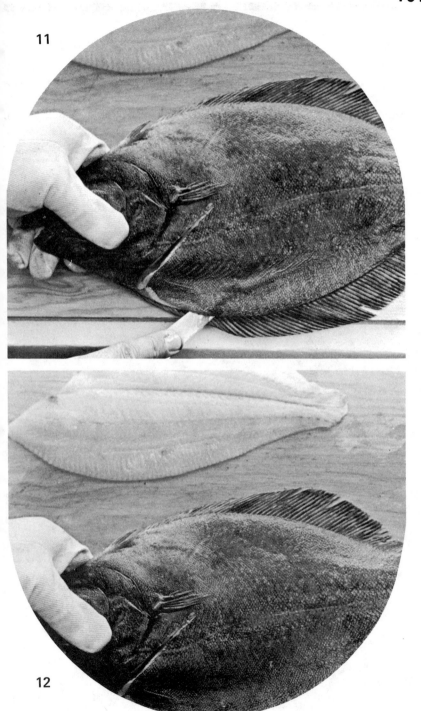

13/14. Start at the tail end of the fish. Hold up the cut part of the fillet, flex the knife tip down to allow it to glide over the backbone and over the rib bones as the cut is made, ending in back of the head. This cut should expose the stomach cavity.

13

14

15/16/17. This cut removes the dark side fillet from the fish. Hold the cut part of the fillet up. Cut behind the stomach cavity down to the backbone and out to the edge of the fish. Turn the knife so it lays flat on the backbone and complete the cut toward the tail, severing the fillet at the tail.

15

16

17

18/19/20. Now, remove the skin from the fillet. Position the fillet with the tail end toward the left. Cut through the flesh to the skin about one inch from the tail end of the fillet. Flatten the knife on the skin and remove the skin from the fillet by making a forward cut while holding the end of the skin down firmly on the board with the fingers. Repeat the same procedure to remove the skin from the other fillet.

18

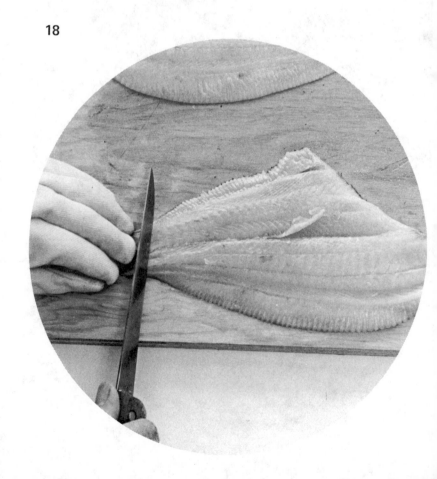

19

20

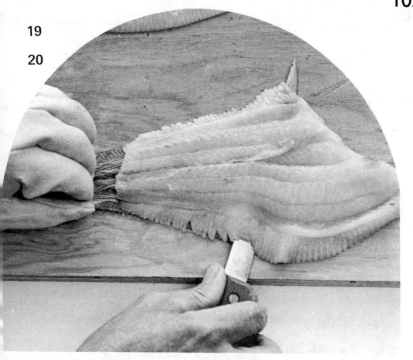

steaking

The following series of illustrations on making "steaks" from large flounder are presented to aid the person, who has some doubts about his filleting ability, in making the most use of his catch.

1/2. With the white side up and head to the left, start the cut through the thick, meaty part directly behind the head of the fish. Continue the cut through the backbone behind the stomach cavity, terminating at the forward end of the anal fin. This cut beheads and virtually eviscerates the fish. Next, follow the same procedures as in No. 2 through 5 for skinners in the previous section. This will remove the tail, anal, and dorsal fins and dark skin from the fish.

3. With the white side down, cut the fish into steaks of the desired width.

1

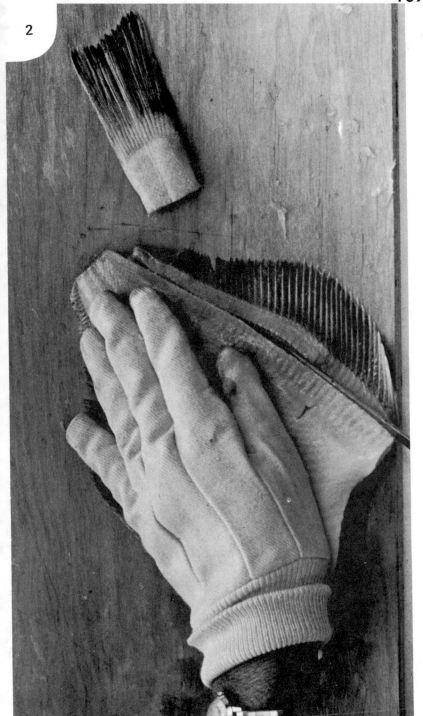

2

3/4. The cut removing the dorsal fin is the most important of all and needs to be made with care. This cut also permits removal of the dark skin on the eyed side of the fish. Start the cut at the forward end of the fish at a slight angle. Cut through the fin bones, but only down to the dark skin. Continue the cut to the end of the tail.

3

4

5/6. Start pulling the dark skin from the fish at the forward end. Get a good grip on both the body of the fish and the fin with the dark skin still attached and peel the dark skin from the fish. The fish is cooked with the white side skin attached.

5

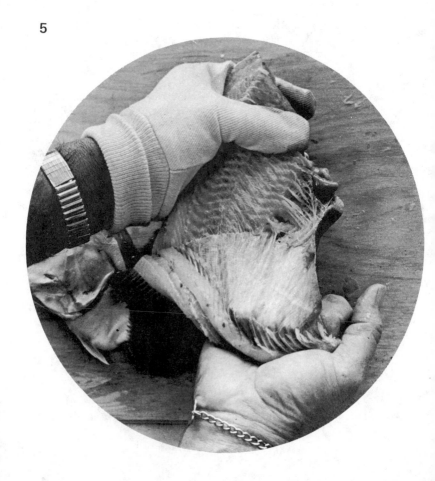

steaking

The following series of illustrations on making "steaks" from large flounder are presented to aid the person, who has some doubts about his filleting ability, in making the most use of his catch.

1/2. With the white side up and head to the left, start the cut through the thick, meaty part directly behind the head of the fish. Continue the cut through the backbone behind the stomach cavity, terminating at the forward end of the anal fin. This cut beheads and virtually eviscerates the fish. Next, follow the same procedures as in No. 2 through 5 for skinners in the previous section. This will remove the tail, anal, and dorsal fins and dark skin from the fish.

3. With the white side down, cut the fish into steaks of the desired width.

1

preparing roundfish

filleting

A salt-water catch will often include several varieties of fish such as lingcod and Pacific cod as well as several different species of rockfish. The filleting procedures for these remarkably different looking fishes are essentially the same. A rockfish is used in the following example as these fishes do present some special considerations. Even when rockfish are dead, the numerous head, dorsal and anal fin spines can painfully wound careless anglers. One of the easiest, quickest, and safest ways to remove the most edible portions of the rockfish is by filleting. A glove for handling the fish is recommended.

1. Lay the fish flat side down on the cutting board with the back to the working edge of the board and with the head on the right.

1

2. Start the first cut at an angle to the head as shown. Cut through the thick, fleshy part directly back of the head down to the backbone.

2

3/4/5. Turn the knife with the flat side up, insert the tip of the blade in the initial cut and cut towards the tail with the flat side of the knife gliding along the backbone. Keep a downward pressure on the knife blade, but do not cut too deep into the fish and sever the rib bones with the knife tip. As the cut is made towards the tail and the blade passes behind the stomach cavity, the blade can be thrust completely through the fish. Continue the cut to sever the fillet at the tail. In continuing the cut, flex the blade downward to allow it to glide over the backbone.

3

4

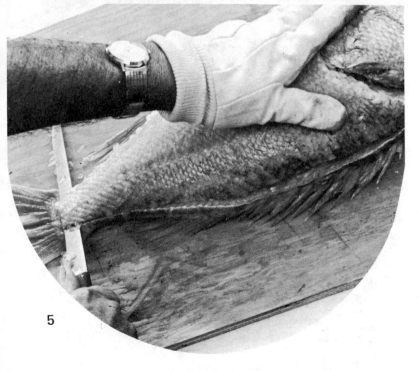

5

6. Hold up the partly severed fillet just behind the ribs and lay the knife blade flat on the backbone. As the cut is made towards the head, exert a

6

downward pressure to flex the blade so it will ride up and over the rib cage to end at the initial cut.

7/8/9. Hold the front part of the fillet up to start the final cut. Direct the line of cut down so the blade will slide over the ribs and the backbone to completely sever the fillet from the fish. Reverse the fish so that the head is to the left with the back to the working edge of the board. The procedures to remove the fillet from this side of the fish are the same as those just presented in No. 2 through 8.

7

8

9

10/11/12. To remove the skin from the fillet, start at a point about one inch from the tail end of the fillet, cut through the flesh to the skin. The bit of flesh on the tail end of the fillet provides a grip on the skin while the flesh is being cut off. Hold the end of the skin down firmly, flatten the blade on the skin and separate the fillet from the skin by making a forward cut.

10

2

3

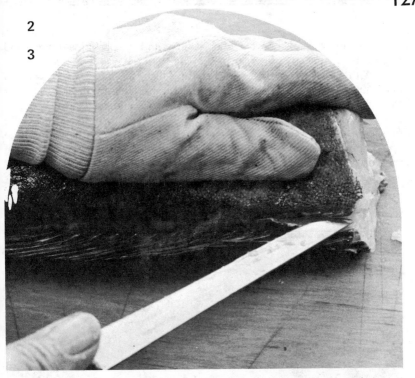

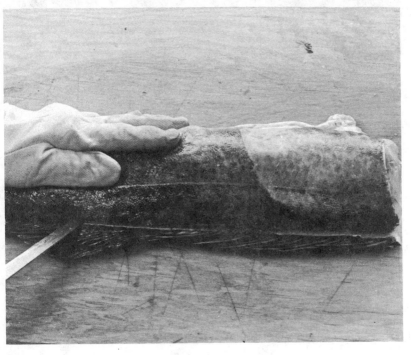

4/5. Grasp the tail end of the dorsal fin against the back side of knife and pull the fin completely out. Trim off the thin stomach wall if desired.

6. With a heavy knife, cut steaks about ½ inch to ¾ inch thick. A wooden block or mallet is often useful in hitting the backside of the knife to cut through the backbone of large fish. When the tail section of the fish becomes too small for steaking, two choice, boneless fillets can be cut from the remaining part of the fish. To remove the first fillet, insert the knife in the center top side of the tail section so that the flat side of the knife slides along the side of the backbone. Exert a downward pressure to keep the flat side of the knife riding the backbone and cut completely through to the groove left by removal of the dorsal fin.

4

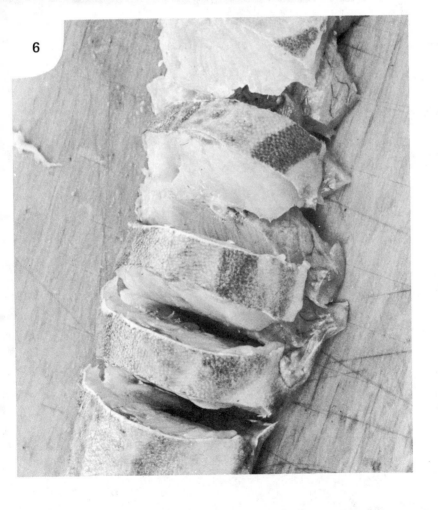

7. Hold the free edge of the fillet up to expose the backbone and with the flat edge of the knife following the backbone, cut in the opposite direction to free the fillet from the backbone.

8/9/10. Leaving the top fillet still attached to the tail section, hold the tail end with the gloved hand and cut through the flesh to the skin. Flatten the knife on the skin and cut the fillet away from the skin by pushing the knife forward.

7

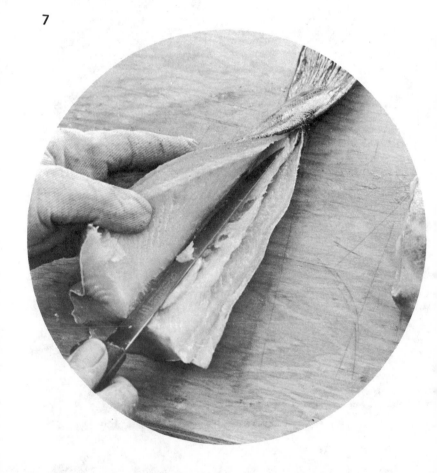

8

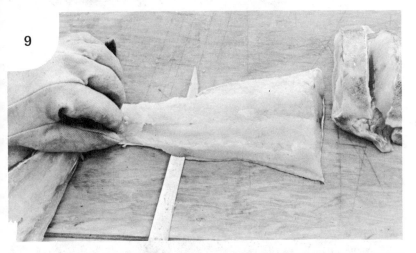

9

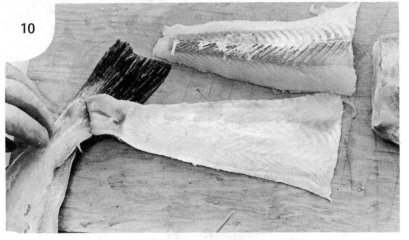

10

11/12. To remove the remaining fillet, insert the knife in the center and under the backbone of the remaining tail section. Continue the thrust so that the flat edge of the knife slides upward against the backbone. With the knife bearing against the backbone, cut to the edge to completely free the one side of the fillet from the backbone. Reverse the cut just described and cut the entire fillet away from the backbone. Remove the skin from this fillet as previously described in No. 9, 10, 11.

11

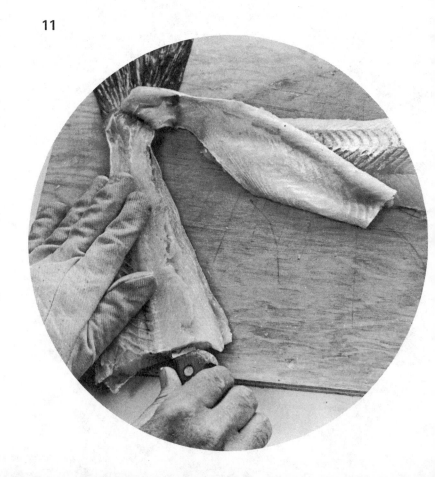

12

preparing salmon

The following procedures for dressing and making a salmon presentable for culinary preparation have been provided for the angler who is fortunate to catch one of the many salmon that abound in the Northwest's waters, but is a bit apprehensive about this "do-it-yourself" task.

A fish can be dressed with head on or head off. The fins can be left on or cut off. For cooking, salmon can be steaked, following the instructions given in the section on steaking roundfish, used half or whole, and split or filleted with virtually all bones removed.

Since salmon are such a highly prized fish, a few hints on their care and cleaning are in order. Immediately upon landing a fish, kill it with a rap on the head with a small club to prevent it from bruising itself by flopping about. Bruises often cause "bloodshot" flesh which must be discarded. Always cool or ice-down your catch and dress the fish as soon as possible. Leaving the entrails in a fish for an extended time, especially during warm weather, will cause "belly burn" to take place inside the fish. This situation is more prevalent in heavily feeding salmon.

If desired, salmon scales can be easily removed with water pressure from a garden hose, provided they haven't been allowed to dry. By directing the water flow from tail to head, a "bright" fish can be descaled in a matter of seconds. If plans call for steaking a salmon after it is dressed, cut off the tail and locate the small blood vessel directly below the vertebrae (backbone). With moderate water pressure, apply the end of the hose directly onto this area, flocing the blood contained in the vessel out into the rear portion of the body cavity. This trick will leave steaks blood free when they are cut. Descaling before cutting also helps give scale-free, attractive steaks.

1/2/3. Starting from the vent (anus), cut through the stomach wall forward toward the head to expose the entrails, ending the cut just past the pectoral fins.

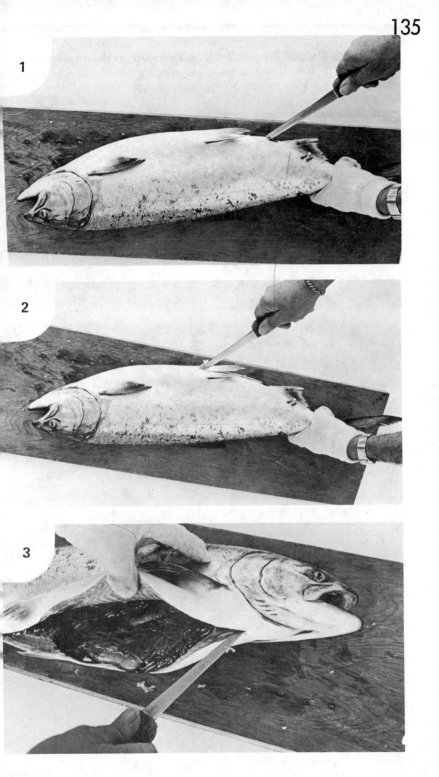

4/5/6/7/8/9. Grasp the gills firmly and cut through the narrow triangular part of the "throat". Continue the cut to sever the gills from the body, while pulling the gills away from the cut. Cut away the gills.

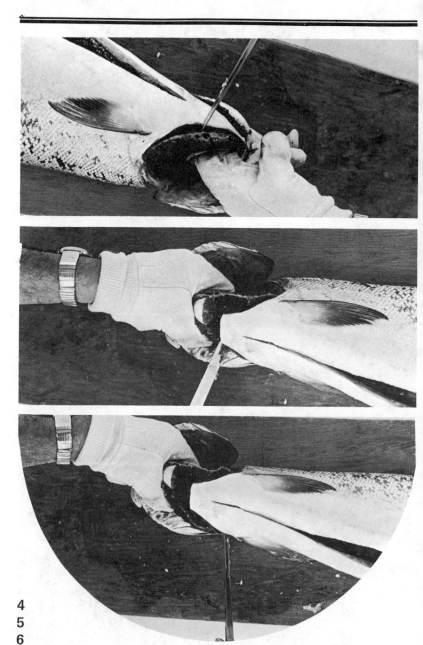

4
5
6

7
8
9

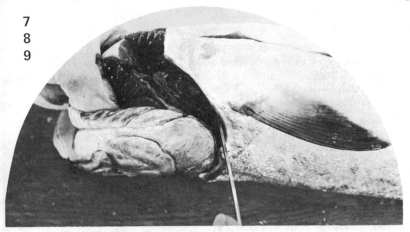

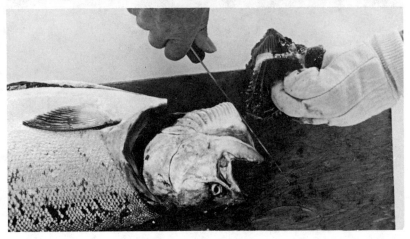

10. Cut the membranes which attach the gullet to the sides of the body wall, cutting completely around as close to the body wall as possible. Grasp the gullet with attached organs and, while pulling towards the tail, remove the entire visceral mass.

11/12/13. The kidney lies along the backbone and appears as a whitish, tapered membrane. This membrane must be cut to remove the kidney — a dark, blood-colored mass. The cut may be directly down the middle, or on either side of the kidney, just inside its attachment to the ribs. The extra cut will allow for complete removal of the membrane and gives a neater appearance to the body cavity of a dressed fish.

10

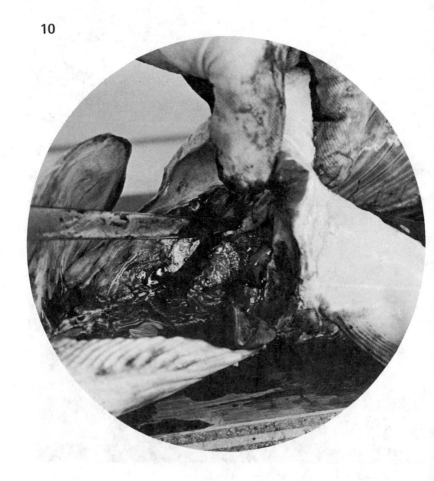

11
12
13

14/15/16/17. Working from head to tail, scrape out the membrane and kidney with a tablespoon. Scrape the area, where ribs join the backbone, vigorously with the tip of the spoon to remove any traces of blood. Wash the body cavity thoroughly and scrape away all remaining tissues to complete the operation for a dressed fish with head on.

14

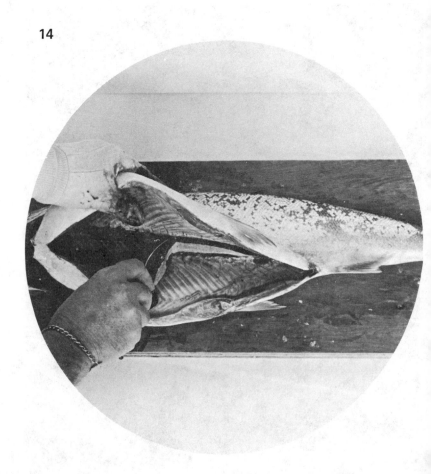

15
16
17

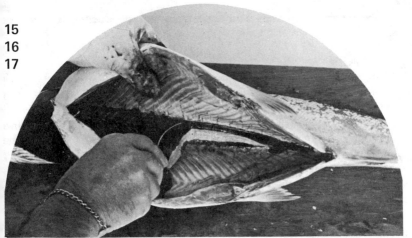

18. To dress the fish, head off, follow the curved contour of the forward part of the fish and cut away the head.

19/20/21/22. Fin removal is optional. This chore requires a very sharp knife. For easier fin removal, cut slightly below the point of fin attachment. If fin removal is desired, doing so before dressing out the fish is much easier especially when cutting off the pelvic and pectoral (belly) fins. These should be removed with a quick, forward thrust of the knife, but use caution!

18

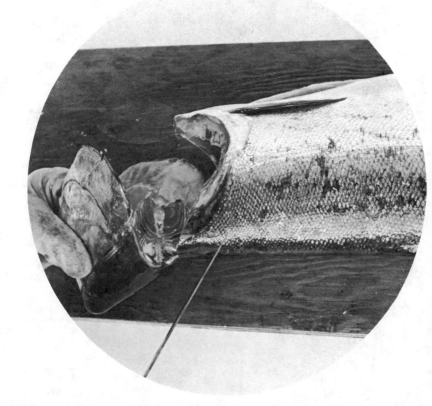

19

20

21

22

filleting

23/24/25. To fillet the salmon, start with the fish dressed, head off. Continue the cut shown in No. 7 to completely sever the remaining attachment of the body walls (at the throat). To remove the first (top) fillet, start the cut at the "head end" of the fish, directly above the backbone (similar to the cut shown in No. 26 for the second fillet). Cut towards the tail, holding the knife flat and firmly against the backbone and, while making this cut, let the knife protrude so that it can be kept following down the center of the back of the fish.

Continue through to the end of the tail.

23

24

25

26/27/28/29/30/31/32. A bit of practice is required to remove the backbone in one cut. These procedures are for the novice, who should use several cuts to remove the backbone and its connected bones without losing too much flesh. With the tip of the knife, start cutting through the ribs at the head end of the fish, keeping the knife's cutting edge always up, toward the backbone. Continue the cut to the end of the body cavity, then cut to the end of the tail. Always keep the cutting edge of the knife gliding along the bones. Continue cutting the backbone from the flesh until the backbone is free.

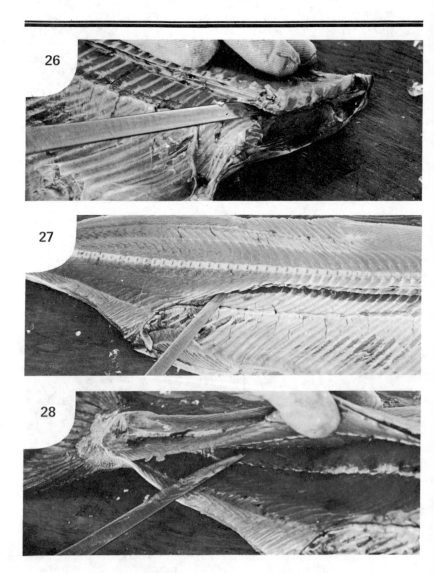

26

27

28

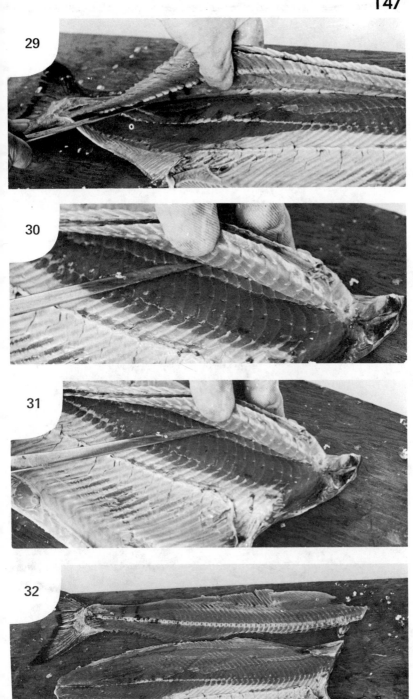

33/34/35/36. Remove the ribs from each fillet by cutting under the ribs with the knife's edge against the bones. Flex the knife downward to follow the rib contour.

33

34
35

36

favorite saltwater fishing areas of oregon

salmon habitat

A first impression, after flying over the West coast's sport fishing fleet, is how very little accessible water is fished. To some extent, this makes sense because salmon are concentrated in specific areas. However, as one learns about fishing, he knows that concentrations of boats often reflect only the attraction that fishermen have for each other. Conversely, a concentration of salmon is often without an accompanying sport fishing fleet.

Fortunately, salmon are, to a large extent, predictable and one's chances of success are greatly enhanced if fishing patterns are recognized and this knowledge is used to select a time and place to fish. The time can relate to season, stage of the tide, or hour.

The importance of selecting a proper time and place for salmon fishing is more critical on bays and other inland waters than off the coast. Salmon near important coastal ports appear to be relatively evenly spread over a broad area. This could result from a rather uniform bottom and shoreline.

Following are maps of Oregon's best saltwater fishing areas.

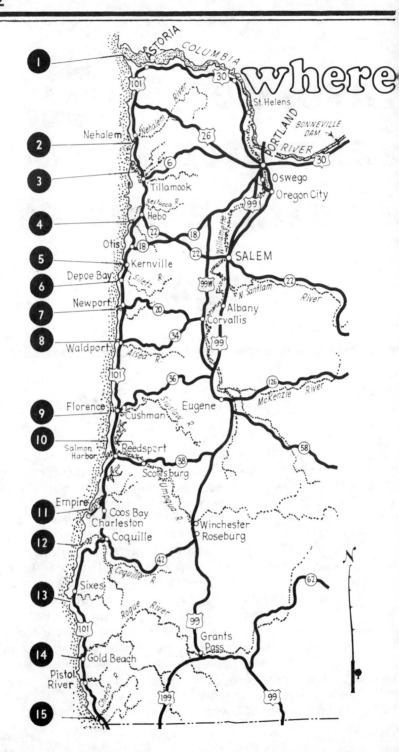

the action is...

fishing maps

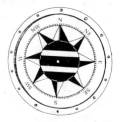

1. Columbia River Mouth
2. Nehalem Bay
3. Tillamook Bay
4. Nestucca Bay and Pacific City
5. Siletz Bay
6. Depoe Bay
7. Yaquina Bay
8. Alsea Bay
9. Siuslaw River and Bay
10. Umpqua River and Winchester Bay
11. Coos Bay
12. Coquille River
13. Port Orford
14. Rogue River at Gold Beach
15. Chetco River

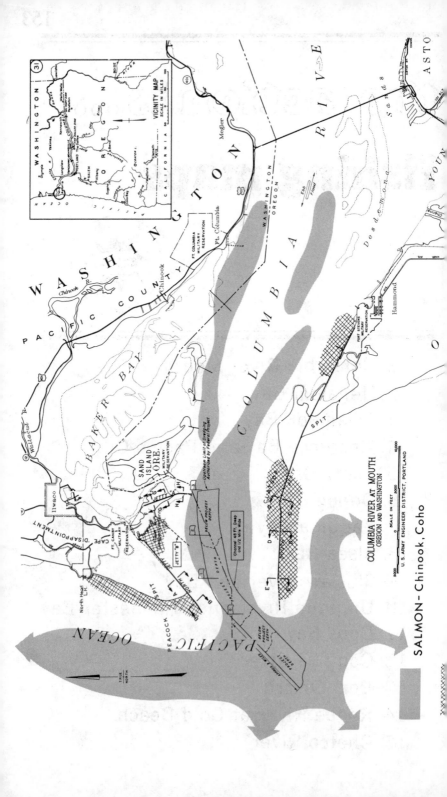

SALMON—Chinook, Coho

1. Columbia River Mouth

Columbia River Jetty "A"

↑ Columbia River North Jetty
Columbia River South Jetty →

COLUMBIA RIVER MOUTH

Mouth of the Columbia is perhaps the most productive sport salmon fishing spot on the Pacific Coast, due primarily to large numbers of coho salmon. Peak fishing period is in August and early September. Smaller feeding chinook and larger spawning-bent chinook are taken during the last three weeks in September, as are numerous coho in the eight to ten pound class. Charter boats are available at Warrenton, Hammond and Astoria, and some search for albacore during summer months 10 to 20 miles offshore.

There is good perch fishing off both north and south jetties, with the south jetty best at elbow on channel side. Yellowtail and widow rockfish, greenling, flounder, lingcod and perch are caught on the ocean side of the south jetty. Rockfish and lingcod are taken around buoys 2 and 4.

Although small boats fish off the Columbia's mouth, water conditions on the bar during ebb tides can be extremely dangerous. There are boat launch facilities at Warrenton, Hammond and Astoria. Ilwaco, on the Washington side, has full charter facilities.

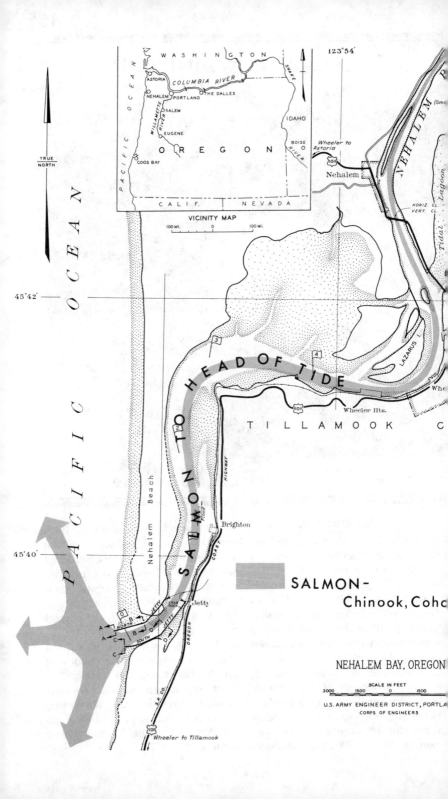

PACIFIC OCEAN

TRUE NORTH

123°54'

45°42'

45°40'

VICINITY MAP

WASHINGTON

COLUMBIA RIVER

SNAKE RIVER

ASTORIA

NEHALEM PORTLAND THE DALLES

WILLAMETTE RIVER

SALEM

IDAHO

EUGENE

BOISE RIVER

OREGON

COOS BAY

CALIF.   NEVADA

100 MI.   0   100 MI.

Wheeler to Astoria

Nehalem

HORIZ. CL.
VERT. CL.

HEAD OF TIDE

Tidal Lagoon

LAZARUS I.

Wheeler Hts.

Wheeler

TILLAMOOK   C

SALMON TO HEAD OF TIDE

Nehalem Beach

HIGHWAY

COAST

Brighton

CRAB ROCK   Jetty

OREGON

S.P. CO.

NORTH   SOUTH JETTY

A B
A C D
C

SALMON-

Chinook, Coho

NEHALEM BAY, OREGON

SCALE IN FEET

3000   1500   0   1500

U.S. ARMY ENGINEER DISTRICT, PORTLAND
CORPS OF ENGINEERS

Wheeler to Tillamook

2. Nehalem Bay

Nehalem River

NEHALEM BAY

Much of the salmon fishing at Nehalem is done inside the bar, since water conditions at the jaws are often very rough. When weather permits, there is excellent chinook and coho fishing outside. The salmon are taken from late August into mid-November, with October usually the peak. Fishing guides may be hired at Nehalem, but they normally fish inside. Besides salmon, there is flounder and perch angling inside the bay. Sloping, sandy beaches on the ocean side limits productive surf fishing, but on calm days flounder, halibut and a variety of rockfish are taken by boaters in the ocean. Most fishermen troll for salmon from near the bar upstream as far as mouth of Foley Creek. Bank anglers and trollers alike catch jack salmon in the river following the first fall rains. These precocious males, both coho and chinook, weigh from three to five pounds and will hit spinners and fresh egg clusters. Boat rentals and boat launching facilities are available.

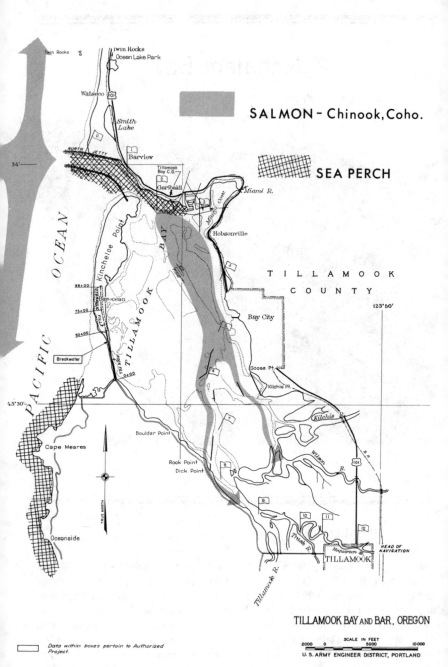

SALMON – Chinook, Coho.

SEA PERCH

Twin Rocks
Ocean Lake Park

Twin Rocks

Watseco

Smith
Lake

NORTH JETTY

34'

Barview

Tillamook
Bay C.G.

Garibaldi

Miami R.

Miami Creek

Hobsonville

OCEAN

Kincheloe Point

TILLAMOOK
COUNTY

123°50'

96+00

73+00

Bayocean

50+00

SOUTH JETTY

Bay City

Breakwater

Goose Pt.

PACIFIC

0+00

Kilchis Pt.

45°30'

Kilchis R.

Boulder Point

Cape Meares

TRUE NORTH

Rock Point
Dick Point

Wilson R.

101

S.P.

Oceanside

Trask R.

Hoquarton Sl.

HEAD OF
NAVIGATION

TILLAMOOK

Tillamook R.

TILLAMOOK BAY AND BAR, OREGON

Data within boxes pertain to Authorized
Project.

SCALE IN FEET
2000   0   5000   10000

U.S. ARMY ENGINEER DISTRICT, PORTLAND

3. Tillamook Bay

Tillamook Bay

Netarts Bay

TILLAMOOK BAY

There is spring chinook salmon fishing in Tillamook Bay from around April 15 to May 15, while fall chinook is best from mid-September to mid-October. Cohos are taken from September through December. Outside salmon fishing is productive during July and August. The bar can be very rough, so small boats may safely cross only in calm weather. There are boat launch facilities and charter services available at Garibaldi and Tillamook.

Fishing for redfin seaperch is good inside the bay around Garibaldi, with fine flounder fishing on the flats.

Some lingcod are caught in deeper water areas inside the bay. Seaperch — redfins, rainbow, silver and dusky — are caught in the ocean surf, while halibut and rockfish, along with salmon, are taken offshore in deeper water.

Just south of Tillamook Bay, separated by Cape Meares, is NETARTS BAY which provides good fishing for flounder and seaperch, along with crabbing and clamming. Greenling, seaperch and rockfish are taken off rocky outcroppings from Cape Lookout to Sand Lake. There is an excellent boat launch site at Netarts.

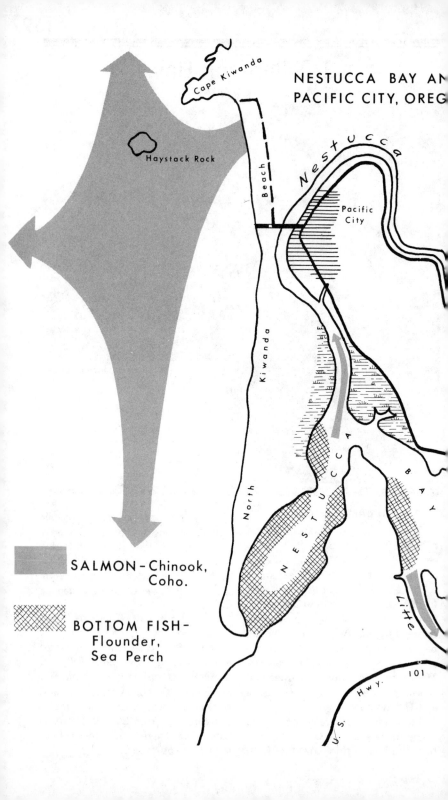

NESTUCCA BAY AN
PACIFIC CITY, OREG

Cape Kiwanda

Haystack Rock

Beach

Nestucca

Pacific
City

Kiwanda

North

NESTUCCA

BAY

Litt

U.S. Hwy. 101

SALMON–Chinook, Coho.

BOTTOM FISH–
Flounder,
Sea Perch

4. Nestucca Bay and Pacific City

NESTUCCA BAY and PACIFIC CITY

Tidewaters of both the Nestucca and Little Nestucca Rivers produce excellent chinook fishing in June and July. The main fall run follows from about the first of August through September. Coho enter the inside catch around September 20 and provide action to the first of December. Spinners and wobblers are favored lures for this inside fishing. Boat rentals and boat launch facilities are available.

Ocean fishing is from Pacific City. New England type dories, about 24 feet long, are launched through the surf. Experienced guides are available here. Salmon fishing in the ocean starts in late June or early July and continues through summer months. There is also excellent fishing for rockfish, lingcod and flounder offshore around reefs and rocky islands. Rock outcroppings at Cape Kiwanda are popular greenling and redfin perch fishing areas.

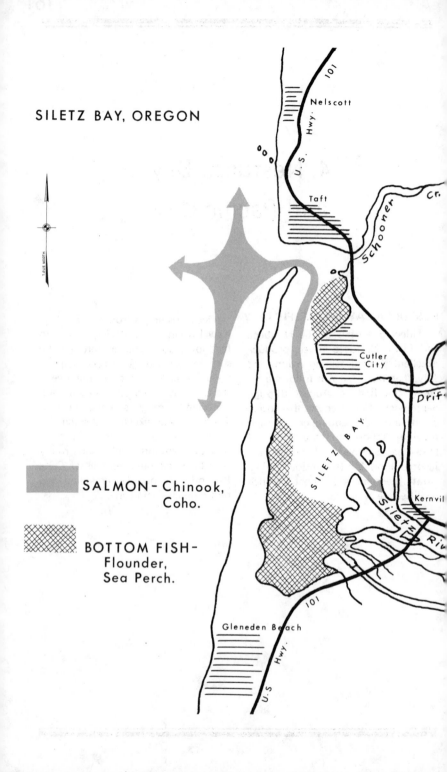

SILETZ BAY, OREGON

TRUE NORTH

Nelscott

U. S. Hwy. 101

Taft

Schooner Cr.

Cutler City

Drif

SILETZ BAY

Siletz Riv

Kernvil

SALMON - Chinook, Coho.

BOTTOM FISH - Flounder, Sea Perch.

Gleneden Beach

U. S. Hwy. 101

5. Siletz Bay

SILETZ BAY

Boaters venture into the ocean out of Siletz Bay in calm weather only, as the bar can be dangerous, and there is considerable salmon fishing inside the bay. When weather permits, anglers find chinook offshore from late June, with coho coming on in August. There is excellent flounder fishing offshore, and seaperch, greenling and rockfish are taken off rock outcroppings along the beach.

Inside fishing begins with sea-run cutthroat in July. These fish provide action into late fall. Large chinook nose into the bay in August with runs peaking in September. Late September is the time for coho to move in. They are at their best in October and November. Most anglers troll for these fish to the head of tide water, although bank casters take all species further upstream by casting spoons or spinners. Tide flats inside the bay provide good flounder fishing, and there is some action on redfin and dusky seaperch from boats. Fishing guides are available, and the area offers boat launching and other marine facilities.

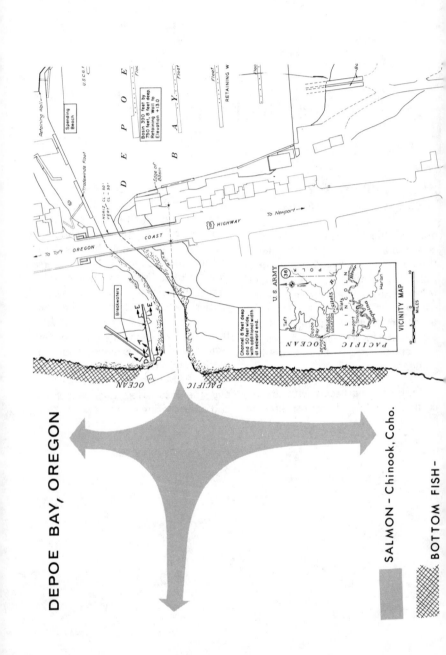

DEPOE BAY, OREGON

SALMON - Chinook, Coho.

BOTTOM FISH -

DEPOE BAY

Basin 390 feet by 750 feet, 8 feet deep. Retaining Wall to Elevation +13.0

Channel 8 feet deep and 50 feet wide, with additional width at seaward end.

HORIZ. CL - 50'
VERT. CL - 50'

Edge of Basin

Spending Beach

U.S.C.G.

Float

Float

RETAINING W

Float

Breakwaters

Oregon COAST HIGHWAY

To Taft
To Newport

PACIFIC OCEAN

VICINITY MAP

U S ARMY

PACIFIC OCEAN

LINCOLN
POLK

Taft
Siletz
Depoe Bay
PROJECT LOCATION
Toledo
Newport
Yaquina
Harlan

MILES

6. Depoe Bay

Depoe Bay

DEPOE BAY

Little inside angling is done at Depoe Bay because of its small size and because there is good, all-weather access to the open sea. There is excellent offshore fishing for several species of rockfish, flounder and lingcod. Reef areas, pinpointed by the charter skippers who work out of Depoe Bay, are highly productive. There is good surf fishing for seaperch, greenling and flounder.

Charters also fish salmon and albacore through summer and early fall months. There is a full range of marine facilities at Depoe Bay.

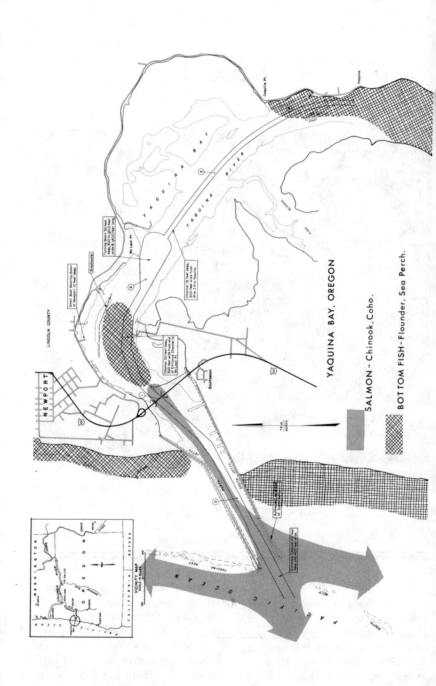

YAQUINA BAY, OREGON

SALMON – Chinook, Coho.

BOTTOM FISH – Flounder, Sea Perch.

7. Yaquina Bay

Yaquina Bay

YAQUINA BAY

Much of the action at Yaquina River's mouth comes from the excellent seaperch fishing inside the bay. The seaperch—redfins, silver, rainbow and dusty—are caught all the way to head of tide. Top areas include along the jetties, at the old Oregon State University Laboratory site, around old pilings on south side of bay and adjacent to boat basins. Herring and candlefish are often abundant inside the bay. Deep water holes inside the bay host lingcod, and flounder are found throughout the bay to head of tide. There is excellent crab fishing inside, also.

Charter boats work out of Yaquina Bay for salmon and albacore. Outside trips start in May and continue through September for chinook and coho salmon. The salmon are caught inside the bay and up the river from August into late fall. Outside fishing for rockfish, flounder and halibut is usually very productive.

Boat launching facilities and rental boats are available.

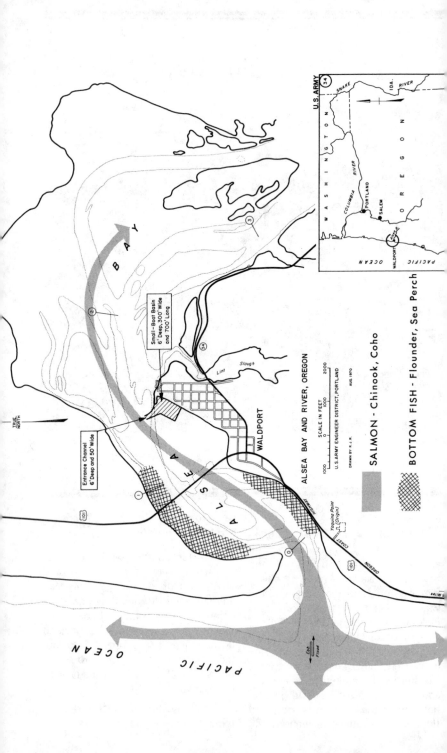

ALSEA BAY AND RIVER, OREGON

SCALE IN FEET

1000   0   1000   2000

U.S. ARMY ENGINEER DISTRICT, PORTLAND

DRAWN BY J.J.R.   AUG. 1970

SALMON - Chinook, Coho

BOTTOM FISH - Flounder, Sea Perch

B A Y

A L S E A

WALDPORT

Slough

Lint

Entrance Channel
6' Deep and 50' Wide

Small-Boat Basin
6' Deep, 300' Wide
and 700' Long

TRUE
NORTH

Yaquina Point
(Origin)

OREGON COAST

PACIFIC   OCEAN

Ebb
Flood

U.S. ARMY

WASHINGTON

OREGON

SNAKE   RIVER

IDA.   RIVER

COLUMBIA   RIVER

Portland

Salem

WALDPORT

PACIFIC   OCEAN

34

8. Alsea Bay

ALSEA BAY

Most salmon fishing takes place inside Alsea Bay because of rough bar conditions and limited fishing guide services. Chinook salmon are taken inside by trolling from the first of August through September, and coho enter the bay in numbers from the middle of September into early November. October is the best month for these sparky salmon. Sea-run cutthroat trout, locally called bluebacks, are caught in the bay and up the river from July to November.

There is good angling for seaperch and flounder in tidal zones. Numerous rock outcroppings along the ocean beach provide cover and good fishing for seaperch, flounder and greenling.

Boats may be launched at various points inside the bay, and rental boats are available.

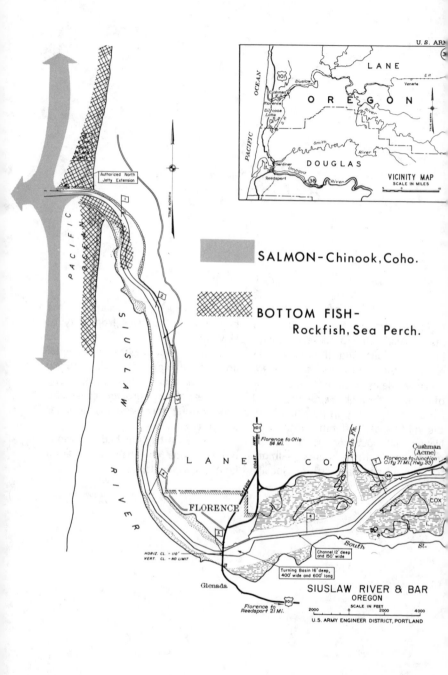

SALMON – Chinook, Coho.

BOTTOM FISH – Rockfish, Sea Perch.

VICINITY MAP
SCALE IN MILES

OCEAN
PACIFIC
LANE
OREGON
DOUGLAS

Siuslaw
Cushman
Florence
Siltcoos Lake
Veneta
S.P.
Smith River
Gardiner
Umpqua River
Reedsport

U.S. ARM

Authorized North Jetty Extension

PACIFIC OCEAN

SIUSLAW RIVER

TRUE NORTH

Florence to Otis 84 Mi.
Cushman (Acme)
Florence to Junction City 71 Mi. (Hwy. 39)

LANE CO.

North Fk.

FLORENCE

COX

South St.

Channel 12' deep and 150' wide

Turning Basin 16' deep, 400' wide and 600' long

HORIZ. CL. - 110'
VERT. CL. - NO LIMIT

Glenada

Florence to Reedsport 21 Mi.

SIUSLAW RIVER & BAR
OREGON

SCALE IN FEET
2000 0 2000 4000

U.S. ARMY ENGINEER DISTRICT, PORTLAND

9. Siuslaw River and Bay

Siuslaw River

SIUSLAW RIVER and BAY

Offshore fishing from the mouth of the Siuslaw River is sometimes limited by rough bar conditions, and this area calls for experienced boatmen. Charter boats are available for salmon fishing in the ocean. Excellent fishing is available inside Siuslaw Bay for seaperch around old docks. Flounder are taken over the tide flats.

Trollers work the bay for coho and chinook salmon, and cutthroat trout from mid-July through November. The section between Florence and Mapleton is most productive, and the peak of salmon fishing comes in September. There are boat launch and other marine facilities along the bay.

Good runs of coho furnish action at nearby Siltcoos and Tahkenitch Lakes during November and December.

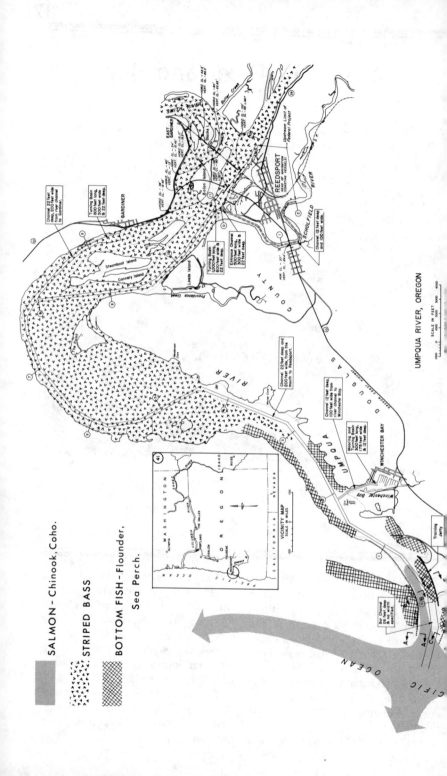

SALMON – Chinook, Coho.

STRIPED BASS

BOTTOM FISH – Flounder,
Sea Perch.

UMPQUA RIVER, OREGON

SCALE IN FEET
1000   0   1000   2000   3000   4000

VICINITY MAP
SCALE IN MILES
100   0   100

PACIFIC OCEAN

10. Umpqua River and Winchester Bay

Umpqua River

Winchester Bay Boat Basin

UMPQUA RIVER and WINCHESTER BAY

Bar conditions at mouth of the Umpqua River permits offshore fishing out of Winchester Bay most of the time. Charter boats run outside from May into September for coho and chinook, with rockfish numerous. Both north and south jetties provide good fishing for redfins, dusky and other seaperch. Flounder and seaperch are taken from the beach in holes along the surf line.

Inside fishing on the Umpqua begins at Winchester and continues upstream to near Roseburg. Spring chinook start in mid-March and continue through June. Fall chinook are available from August into September, while coho enter the river following the first heavy fall rains. Fishing guides and charters work inside as well as offshore. There are boat launch sites and a wide range of other facilities at Salmon Harbor near the town of Winchester Bay.

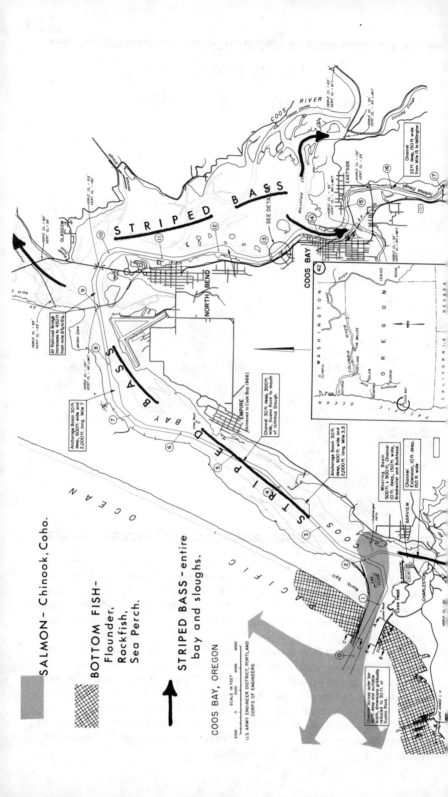

11. Coos Bay

Coos Bay

Charleston Boat Basin

COOS BAY

Jetties provide excellent protection for boaters crossing the bay from Coos Bay into the ocean. Charter boats work offshore for chinook and coho, along with bottom fish, from early June to early September. There are public boat mooring and boat launch facilities at Charleston, just inside the bar. Headlands along the ocean provide good fishing spots for seaperch, greenling, flounder and rockfish.

Excellent redfin seaperch angling is available along the jetties, on the inside south arm to Charleston, and up the bay past North Bend. These same areas also produce flounder. Striped bass are caught throughout the entire bay and sloughs. (See separate striped bass story.)

There isn't much inside angling for salmon except near the head of tide from around September 15 to November 1 when the fish gang to wait for a surge of fresh water to send them upstream to spawning grounds.

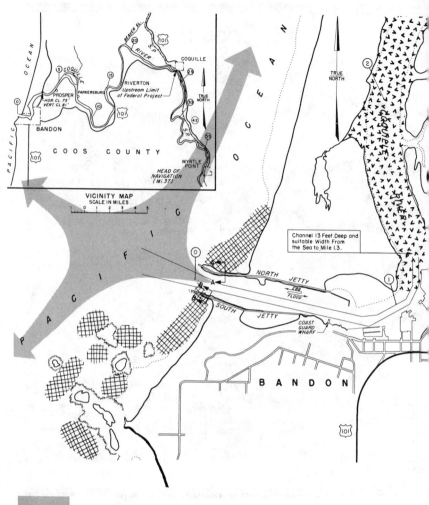

VICINITY MAP
SCALE IN MILES
0 1 2 3 4 5

OCEAN

PACIFIC

COOS COUNTY

OCEAN

TRUE
NORTH

Channel 13 Feet Deep and
suitable Width From
the Sea to Mile 1.3.

NORTH JETTY

EBB
FLOOD

SOUTH JETTY

COAST
GUARD
WHARF

BANDON

SALMON - Chinook, Coho.

BOTTOM FISH-
Rockfish-Sea Perch.

STRIPED BASS

COQUILLE RIVER, ORE

SCALE IN FEET
1000   0   1000

U.S. ARMY ENGINEER DISTRICT, PORT

DRAWN BY: S.H.B., R.J.R.   SE

12. Coquille River

Coquille River

COQUILLE RIVER

Rough water conditions at the mouth of the Coquille River, despite protective jetties, sometimes restrict offshore fishing. Both chinook and coho enter this river, and they are taken off the mouth in the ocean from June into September. Offshore reefs and rocky islands provide excellent habitat for a variety of bottom fish including rockfish, flounder, lingcod and abundant cabezon.

Salmon fishing inside the river's mouth starts around mid-September and continues until the first high water in November. Fishing is done upstream for about 20 miles. Angling for seaperch is productive along the jetties and upstream for several miles. There is a good striped bass fishery in sloughs off the Coquille. (See separate striped bass story.)

Boat ramps are situated at various points along the tidewater area.

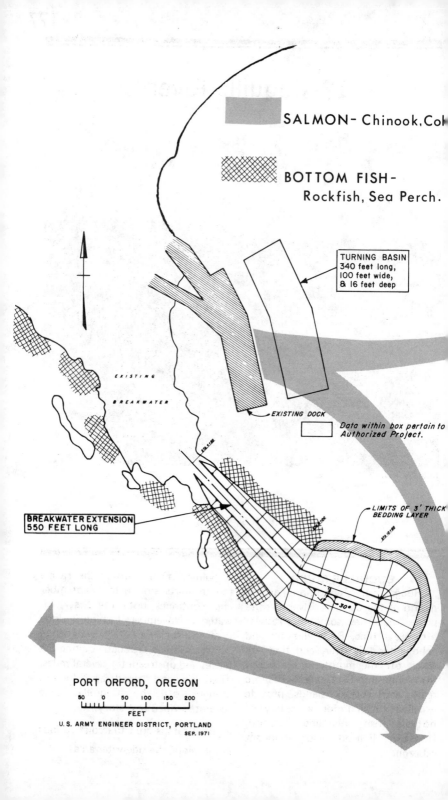

SALMON- Chinook, Col

BOTTOM FISH-
Rockfish, Sea Perch.

TURNING BASIN
340 feet long,
100 feet wide,
& 16 feet deep

EXISTING

BREAKWATER

EXISTING DOCK

Data within box pertain to
Authorized Project.

LIMITS OF 3' THICK
BEDDING LAYER

BREAKWATER EXTENSION
550 FEET LONG

30°

PORT ORFORD, OREGON

50   0   50   100   150   200
FEET

U.S. ARMY ENGINEER DISTRICT, PORTLAND
SEP. 1971

13. Port Orford

Port Orford

PORT ORFORD

The boat basin in this small harbor is protected by a sweeping cape headland. Chinook and coho are taken from this area from June into September, but there is no river emptying into the harbor, thus the fish are feeding salmon. There are limited charter fishing services.

Rocky headlands, interrupted by beautiful sandy beaches, offer excellent fishing. Almost any outcropping or hole along the beach will produce redfins, silver, rainbow or dusky seaperch, and greenling are abundant among the reefs. Flounder fishing in the Port Orford area is rated good.

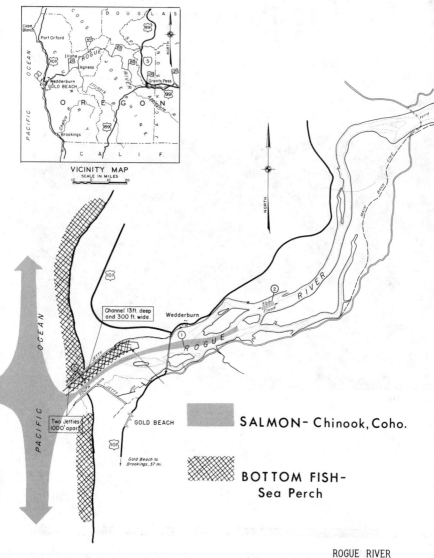

VICINITY MAP

SCALE IN MILES

10 0 10 20

Channel 13ft. deep
and 300 ft. wide.

Wedderburn

ROGUE

RIVER

Ebb
Flood

Two Jetties
1000' apart

GOLD BEACH

Gold Beach to
Brookings, 37 mi.

PACIFIC

OCEAN

NORTH

SALMON– Chinook, Coho.

BOTTOM FISH–
Sea Perch

ROGUE RIVER
HARBOR AT GOLD BEACH, OREG.

SCALE IN FEET

2000   1000   0   2000   4,000

U.S. ARMY ENGINEER DISTRICT, PORTLAND

14. Rogue River at Gold Beach

Rogue River

ROGUE RIVER at GOLD BEACH

Charter facilities are excellent at the Rogue River's mouth at Wedderburn on the north side and at Gold Beach on the south side. The bar can be rough, but offshore fishing for salmon, rockfish, greenling and lingcod is productive. Ocean fishing for salmon is done from mid-July through September. Rocky headlands, both north and south of the Rogue, provide good bottomfish angling, and surf fishing can be excellent along Nesika Beach and off Ophir at mouth of Enchre Creek.

River fishing from boats in the lower Rogue is both popular and productive. Salmon fishing gets under way in April for spring chinook and continues into December for coho, with many heavy fall chinook taken in July and August. Trolling with spinners is an effective fishing method inside the river.

There is a wide range of marine and tourist facilities at Wedderburn and Gold Beach, with boat launch ramps just inside the river mouth.

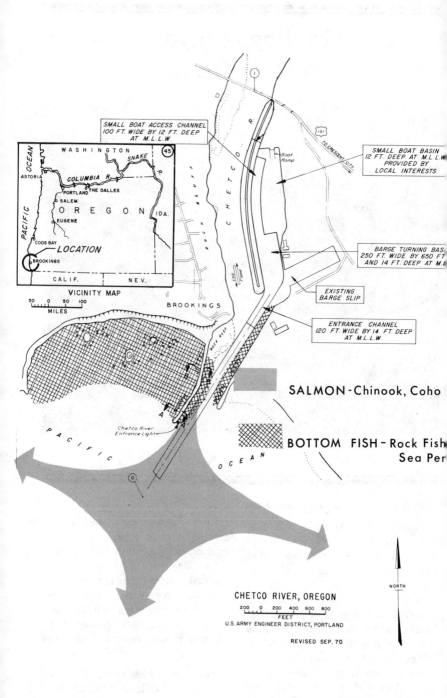

SMALL BOAT ACCESS CHANNEL
100 FT. WIDE BY 12 FT. DEEP
AT M.L.L.W.

45

SMALL BOAT BASIN
12 FT. DEEP AT M.L.L.W.
PROVIDED BY
LOCAL INTERESTS

Boat Ramp

TO CRESCENT CITY

BARGE TURNING BAS
250 FT. WIDE BY 650 FT
AND 14 FT. DEEP AT M.I

EXISTING
BARGE SLIP

ENTRANCE CHANNEL
120 FT. WIDE BY 14 FT. DEEP
AT M.L.L.W.

ROCK BLUFF

CHETCO R.

EBB FLOOD

BROOKINGS

ROCK REEF

Chetco River
Entrance Light

PACIFIC

OCEAN

SALMON - Chinook, Coho

BOTTOM FISH - Rock Fish
Sea Per

Vicinity Map (inset):

WASHINGTON

SNAKE R.

COLUMBIA R.

ASTORIA

THE DALLES

PORTLAND

SALEM

O R E G O N

EUGENE

IDA.

COOS BAY

LOCATION

BROOKINGS

PACIFIC OCEAN

CALIF.   NEV.

VICINITY MAP

50   0   50   100
MILES

CHETCO RIVER, OREGON

200   0   200   400 600 800
FEET
U.S. ARMY ENGINEER DISTRICT, PORTLAND

REVISED SEP. 70

NORTH

15. Chetco River

Chetco River

Chetco Boat Basin

CHETCO RIVER

Heavy runs of chinook and coho enter the Chetco and provide good fishing both offshore and at the river's mouth. Offshore chinook fishing begins in July, and best coho angling is during August and September. There is a small harbor at Brockings with limited boat facilities and some charter service.

Chinook enter the Chetco from September into mid-November, while coho move in from late September through December. Trolling is popular in tidewater, but salmon are caught by bank anglers further up the river.

Chetco Cove at the north jaw of the river has numerous submerged rocks and provides excellent fishing for seaperch, rockfish, lingcod, greenling and other species. Rocky headlands along this stretch of coast provide habitat for a wide variety of bottom fish which may be caught from the beach.

STRIPED BASS!

by MILT GUYMON

Fish culturist Livingston Stone had faint hopes that the 132 small striped bass, sole survivors of a slow, cross-country journey from the Atlantic Seaboard to the Pacific Coast, would be the forerunners of a major sport fishery when he released the little fingerlings into San Francisco Bay. The time was in the 1870's and it is amazing that any survived at all in view of the poor transportation and fish handling facilities of the day.

But the success of this small plant of striped bass was soon observed by both sport and commercial fishermen. The little bass obviously found conditions in the Pacific much to their liking — both for growth and reproduction — and they soon spread to drainages to the north.

Adult stripers moved up along the Oregon coast, but found conditions unfavorable north of the central coastal area. Although an occasional striper is taken as far north as the Columbia, the species appears to be confined to certain estuaries south of the Siuslaw River.

Striped bass may remain in fresh or brackish water for their entire life, but most migrate to the ocean, spending the winter along the surf, and return in early spring to freshwater estuaries to spawn.

These big ocean fish live to a respectable age as compared to trout or salmon. Scale samples from large fish caught at Coos Bay show that some may live upward to 20 years or more. These old timers often exceed 50 pounds in weight. Fish to 60 pounds are not uncommon. The Oregon record is one of 63 pounds caught in the Umpqua in early May. Fish from 20 to 40 pounds are common in Oregon waters.

When Oregon anglers discuss striped bass fishing, the hot spots center in the Coquille, Coos Bay and the Umpqua. In March in some years, large numbers move into the Siuslaw tidal zone, but it appears the schools are on feeding forays which seldom last more than a month.

COQUILLE — The Coquille is fished lighter than either Coos Bay or Umpqua. Yet, the striped bass in this system are numerous and average large. The fish concentrate in the Riverton area and most angling takes place between the boat ramp and the ferry landing. Coquille stripers are spooky and tougher to catch than in other estuaries.

On this river anglers fish almost entirely on the spawning run, which extends from early March into June. The lower bay contains bass during the summer, but it has never really been explored by fishermen.

COOS BAY — In the Coos system,

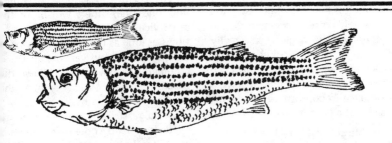

anglers work tidal portions of the Millicoma and South Fork Coos Rivers where bass concentrate to spawn. The upstream movement varies and is unpredictable. Generally, the runs work upstream in late February or early March and peak in April and May.

Popular area for trolling include the sections from Landreth Bridge to Bessie Creek and from Dellwood to the Menasha log dump. Deep running plugs, such as Beno Eels, Jug-a-doo Eels, jointed Creek Chub and Rebels are most productive.

In June and through the rest of the summer, anglers follow the bass down to the tide flats where the fish move to feed. Both bank and boat angling are pursued. Surface poppers, streamer flies, and bait are all used with success. Casters work the mouths of Kentuck, Haynes, and North Sloughs with Rebel poppers or Lucky 13 plugs. Other concentration points for stripers are the Menasha Fill and near the North Bend Airport.

Plunkers use bait floated under a bobber in the shallow flats and the deeper channels. Mouths of the various sloughs are most productive since bass move in and out with the tides.

UMPQUA RIVER — Stripers follow the smelt run into the Umpqua, generally in February, March and April. Most angling at this time takes place near the head of tide, some 25 miles upstream. Rebel plugs and Jig-a-doo Eels are the better lures.

From May through summer, the bass move to the lower tide flats and concentrate in the Big Bend area to Schofield Creek.

On the Smith River, lower Umpqua tributary, anglers troll mostly in the Noel Ranch area during early spring, then move to the marshy islands near the mouth in late spring and summer.

SURF FISHING POTENTIAL

A relatively untapped striped bass sport fishery exists for the adventurous angler along the coast. Oregon anglers have not explored the surf fishing potential, but have concentrated their efforts almost entirely to the estuaries. Nontheless, the striper is a surf fish and comes in close to the beach to feed. When he's not in the bays on spawning runs he's in the ocean feeding along the coastal shelf.

The normal procedure is to find the "holes" along the beach, an area where a gentle, sloping sand beach suddenly deepens close to the shore forming a deep water pocket. The angler casts into or at the edge of the pocket, places his rod in a sandspike, and waits for a striped bass to come along. Schools of stripers feed in or just outside the breakers and will turn into these pockets as they follow the shelf. Bass are also attracted to these pockets by food fish which often concentrate in these holes. The angler can readily identify such a pocket by its appearance — generally blue-green water with a minimum of wave disturbance in contrast to the rolling breakers of adjacent surf.

NEED HUSKY GEAR

A good outfit is required, one capable of casting weights from four to six ounces. Pyramid sinkers are best as these will stick in the sand, while rounded ones will roll in the surf. The sinker is fastened to the terminal end of a three or four-foot leader. Two dropper hooks are spaced above and high enough to keep the bait off the bottom. Hooks should be fairly large, at least 2/0 or better.

Baits are many, but the most productive are squid, small crabs, and bait fish. Herring and candlefish are excellent. Use small bait fish whole, but cut the large ones into chunks about three or four inches in length. The best success will be had on the head and tail sections. Thread the bait on the hook well as crabs and surf perch are adept at bait stealing. The angler must watch the tides and do his fishing on the incoming flow and continue until the runoff is about half over, or until the pocket becomes too shallow.

Casting lures, flies or baits is also effective in taking stripers in the surf. Best bet is to retrieve at a medium-fast rate of speed. Retrieve at a steady pace instead of jerking the lure or fly as one would for black bass.

Both shallow and deep-running plugs are good for surf casting. Streamer flies will produce, especially those in white, yellow or blue colors.

Stripers run in schools, so where you find one, others will be in the same vicinity. Action can be fast at times as long as the school remains in feeding areas. However, the striper is a nomad and moves up and down the beach following or in search of the food on which he dines.

A big striper is much more difficult to land in the surf than he is in the quieter waters of bays and inlets. His strategy in the ocean is to swim crosswise of the surf, using the powerful undertows or outflowing tidal wave as added leverage against the angler's rod.

Only a handful of sport fishermen work striped bass in the surf. These fishermen have a good thing going for themselves the year around. Winter is the best time since many mature fish will be in the bays on spawning runs from early spring to mid-summer. But there's still large schools of stripers outside as well. And when the stripers quit the estuaries in late summer to return to the surf, there's a bonanza of exciting action available to the angler who will seek it out.

FISHING TECHNIQUES

Striped bass may be taken at night as well as day. Night angling is the most popular and productive. It is also the most exciting, especially using surface lures or flies. Anglers can also hear feeding bass much more clearly at night than he can in the daytime. Daytime fishing is also productive, but stripers are more difficult to locate and they are much more spooky.

Striper movement is keyed to the tides. High and low slack are best. On the flood bass move onto the flats to feed then return to deeper water with the ebb. Successful anglers watch for fish movements at all tide periods.

Many baits and lures are used to take stripers. Cut bait and herring are popular. The most productive methods are to cast or troll both surface or underwater plugs. Rebel and Sea-bees are effective lures as are artificial eels and squid. Jointed plugs are excellent. Most anglers use regular steelhead or salmon mooching or fly rods to adequately handle the big fish.

Both trolling and anchor fishing methods are utilized by boaters. An effective method is to cruise slowly on the incoming tide and scout for feeding schools. Stripers spend a lot of time at or near the surface and can readily be observed feeding on the surface or as a dark shadow or cloud underwater as the pod of fish move about. Look for swirls, boils or "wakes" made by moving fish. Frequently, bass will chase bait fish into the air or up on the beach.

When a school is spotted the angler moves ahead, drops anchor, and casts lure or fly to the oncoming fish. When the school passes the boat is moved ahead to again intercept. Motors must not be used within two or three-hundred feet of a feeding school or the fish will sound.

Work the tide flats or lower tips of islands for best success. On the outgoing tide look for points or tips of islands where the current comes together. Bait fishermen do best at drop-offs at the mouth of channels.

FLY FISHING POPULAR

Fly fishing for stripers is a popular method, gaining in popularity each year. A good fly fisherman will take more fish on the average than will a good troller or bait fisherman. Maribou streamers are excellent, as are the large streamers used for coho. Three to six-inch streamers will produce, with those 3½ to 4-inches the most productive.

Large flies are difficult to cast, especially in the coastal winds. It also requires a strong arm to handle the heavy-duty fly rod and heavy line necessary to make long casts, as well as to handle a strong-running striper. The rod should be at least 9 feet in length, and the line must be at least number 10 with sinking shooting head. Use lots of backing. The fly is retrieved very fast. Bucktail jigs are used with some success, and feathered jigs are excellent. However, the striper is a vicious feeder and the feathers will be pretty well mutilated after one or two attacks.

SUGGESTED TACKLE

As mentioned, most anglers use regular steelhead or salmon mooching, casting or fly rods. Regular surf rods are best for the surf, but anglers can get by with 8½ or 9-foot casting rods.

Lures should include two or three big poppers such as Rebel, Lucky 13, Heddon Basser; two or three floating or swimming plugs, such as Rebel, Rappulas, jointed plugs; Six or eight trolling plugs such as Jig-a-doo Eels, Beno Eels, deep diving Rebels, or other sinking lures about 7½ inches in length. A good selection of jigs, ¼ to 1-ounce, in various colors should be carried, and a variety of streamers, 3 to 6 inches in length should be included. A supply of bait hooks, 3/0 - 4/0, and an assortment of clamp on, pyramid, or other weights, ½ to 4-ounces, are necessary.

LURE COLORS

Plugs in blue and silver, blue and white, red and white, perch scale are best, with dark colors for night fishing. Jigs and streamers in yellow, yellow and white, blue and yellow, blue, green, or combination of colors, and eels in green, pale blue or black, are most productive.

CHUM, CHINOOK, SOCKEYE, SILVERS, HUMPY!!

Northwest's river-run salmon

Salmon fishing is not restricted to salt water areas of the Pacific Northwest, as most major, and many minor, streams tributary to the ocean carry at least some of the five species of Pacific salmon. In lower reaches of larger rivers, particularly, bright salmon are taken by sports anglers trolling from boats with spoons, spinners, plugs or herring, and by bank fishermen who use the same terminal gear plus eggs.

Winter steelhead-type fishing gear is commonly used by bank fishermen, while standard salmon gear is utilized by boaters who troll.

Stan Jones Photo

Species of salmon furnishing most fresh water action include fall and spring or summer chinook, cohos and humpies (pinks). The humpies run only in odd-numbered years and their range is primarily north of the Columbia river, while chinook and coho make annual runs. Probably most fresh water action from salmon is provided by jack chinook and jack coho. Jacks are two-year-old salmon, almost invariably males, which mature early and return to native streams. They are capable of spawning and often are present in large numbers.

Occasionally stream fishermen will catch chum and sockeye salmon, the other two species of salmon found in Northwest rivers. These salmon do not often hit lures of bait even when present in large numbers.

salmon are found in

deeper runs!

Salmon are found in a bit different type water than steelhead. They usually favor slower and deeper runs. Coho and humpy salmon, particularly, are often active and do considerable rolling and jumping in rivers when stacked in holes. Some fishermen locate rolling fish before settling down to serious fishing.

Here are some hints which should help:

COHO SALMON. (Adult) Fish the deep, slack water which contains cover such as logs, rocks, over-hanging brush or under-cut banks. This is the type water that holds sea-run cutthroat. Watch for rolling fish and pitch golf tee spinners, large spinners, winged bobbers or colorful wobbling spoons. Silvers will sometimes pick up eggs and yarn offerings. Medium weight steelhead tackle is ideal.

CHINOOK SALMON. (Adult) These fish are found close to the heavy current line in deeper water. They should be fished deep and slow. Spring chinook may be found a bit higher in the pool than the riper fall chinook. Winged bobbers, large spinners, wobbling spoons and eggs and yarn will take them. Sometimes fresh prawns are used effectively. Because of the chance of hooking giant chinook, heavy steelhead gear is in order.

HUMPY SALMON. These salmon commonly gang in deep pools and are often very active. Tiny wobblers, fished deep and slow, will entice them, as will small spinners.

JACK SALMON. (Chinook and Coho) The jacks are found with adult salmon, and also frequent riffles. Cluster eggs are probably the most effective bait, but spinners and spoons will take them. Light spinning gear will handle jacks.

RIVER GEAR

6 TO 20 LB. NYLON

SPOON

SPINNER

"BOBBER" TYPE LURE

SALMON OR STEELHEAD

Wash. State Fisheries

Fish The Surf

Many of the Northwest's sandy beaches fronting the ocean offer good to excellent surf fishing, although relatively few anglers try it. There are a dozen or more species of surf perch, the principal fish caught from Northwest beaches, with the red-tail or red-fin variety providing most of the action.

Surf Fishing In Strait of Juan de Fuca

The red-tail perch may reach 18 inches and five pounds, but 12 inchers are more common. Sea perch are unusual in that they give birth to live young. The fish live in schools and feed on mussels, marine worms, crustaceans and other marine life. Their flesh is white and very good eating.

Secret of successful surf perch fishing is to find feeding grounds. Food gathers in holes or troughs in the beach and perch concentrate at these spots. Inexperienced fishermen will probably do best by walking the beach at low tide to spot likely holes, then fish them on the in-tide. Holes may be located by watching for flat or slick spots in the first row of breakers. Perch may also be taken on out-tides. They may be caught all year long.

Jetties and rocks provide excellent fishing spots for perch and other fish as they offer easy access to deep water.

Surf fishing is easy. Merely cast into the surf where there is some sign of a hole, let the bait sink to the bottom, and pick up slack line. Perch are active and there is no doubt about strikes if the line is tight.

Clam necks, mussels, shrimp, pile worms, ghost shrimp or small spoons are effective bait. Large spinning or casting reels, holding about 200 yards of 15 pound test, are ideal. Husky rods of eight to ten foot length should be used. Typical leader set-up includes two loops for dropper hooks, with a swivel to the line and a snap swivel on the other end of the 12 pound test leader for the sinker. Leader of 15 to 24 inches works fine. Sinkers are two to six ounce, with four ouncers most common. Hooks are rather small; sizes four, six or eight, depending on size of the bait. bait.

Beaches at Westport, Ocean Shores, Long Beach, Klaloch, Copalis and Tokeland in Washington are among the many good surf fishing areas in the state.

Top areas in Oregon include south jetty of Columbia River, Garibaldi, Sandlake, Siletz, beach heads adjacent to Yaquina Bay and inside the bay.

Other species of fish caught from the Northwest's beaches, jetties and rocks include rockfish, ling cod, flat fish such as flounder, and an occasional salmon.

a really secret way to barbeque FISH

So you caught a steelhead or salmon and have proudly flopped the dead fish on your wife's clean drainboard. As long as there are scales all over the kitchen and you still reek of the great conquest, why not put the knife to the fish and prepare it for a pleasant evening barbeque?

Sharpen the knife, make a cut along the gill cover as deep as the backbone, then carefully work the blade of a limber fillet knife along the backbone. You should come up with a slab of meat from both sides with most of the bones remaining on the carcass of the fish.

If the barbecue party is a week or so away, con a cake pan from the woman you live with and place the fillets therein. Then fill the pan with water, covering all the fish. After the fish is frozen, pull the pan out and give it a sharp rap. Presto, you now have a cake of ice with the fish enclosed which may be easily stacked in the freezer.

Pull the fish from the freezer the night before B-Day and lay in a supply of heavy aluminum foil and charcoal. Fire up the barbecue unit well in advance to insure that coals cover the entire bottom of the rig.

Make a dish of the aluminum foil the same size as the top of your barbecue unit, making a lip of about one inch all around so that all juices will be retained. Then cut the fish into serving pieces. Grease the grill on the barbecue unit, then place the fish, flesh side down, on the grill close to the coals. The idea is a quick sear job.

Thus far it has been all man work, but the gal should have been working in the kitchen all this time doing this:

Madam will take 1/2 lb. margarine, 1 cup water, 1-1/2 cup tomato juice, 1/3 T. dry mustard, 3/4 T. salt, 3/4 T. sugar, 3/4 T. chili powder, 1/2 T. Worcestershire sauce, 1/2 T. tabasco, 3/4 T. black pepper, 1 T. paprika, 1/4 cup vinegar, 1 grated onion, 1 clove garlic. She will combine all ingredients and simmer for 30 minutes. If madam is real smart she will make a double or triple batch while she is at it (freeze the surplus) because this is a helluva lot of messing around. But worth it! The above will make about one quart, enough for one large fish.

Are those chunks of fish browning nicely? OK, use a flapjack turner and place them, flesh side up, in the foil pan you've fashioned. Then raise the grill away from coals and place the pan and fish back over the fire. Here comes madam with the Cowboy Sauce. Whoopee! The fillets of fish will have cracks from the sear-job. Start spooning the sauce into the cracks and all over the fish. Keep spooning.

Are you still on the sauce? Keep basting until the fish is ready to be served. If you have plenty of fish not much more will be needed, but you might serve fruit or tossed salad, corn on the cob, garlic bread and coffee, tea or booze.

And that, fellow anglers, makes tremendous eating. After your wife has tried it she may relinquish custody long enough for you to make another fishing trip.

—STAN JONES—

Zap Silvers With Flies !

IT'S THE ONLY WAY TO TROLL

Coho fly fishing for coho salmon is probably the most sporty method known to take these acrobatic fish. The terminal equipment is simple—just a large bucktail fly—but this technique will often produce when herring or flashers pull the skunk.

The fly, commonly called a coho fly, is tied to the end of a mono line of 10 to 15 pound test and trailed behind a boat. That's it. No lead, no swivel. Just hang the fly out there 20 to 40 feet behind the boat right on all fishing, a needle-sharp point on your hook is imperative.

Fly fishing for coho in Oregon waters has not yet gained wide popularity, but knowledgeable fishermen believe they can be taken in most of the state's ocean areas.

One of the top areas for fly fishing for coho in Washington waters is at mouth of Strait of Juan de Fuca out of Neah Bay. Schools of coho from many river systems gang here in the late summer and fall months before heading up or down

COHO FLY

½ ACTUAL SIZE

the edge of the motor wake. Trolling is fast, so fast that ideally the fly will create a rooster tail or "V" on the surface of the water.

Coho salmon will attack from any side and are often seen flashing short. It takes an iron-nerved fisherman to resist setting the hook when it appears as though the coho is climbing all over his fly. The best technique involves placing your rod in a rod holder or bracing it securely so that a strike won't yank the outfit out of the boat. Set the drag loose. Then stand or sit back from your rod with your hands in your pockets. Really, put your hands in your pockets. When a coho sizzles in he'll inhale the fly, turn and be on his way before the fastest reacting angler can grab the fishing stick. This is good because **after** he has turned with the fly is the time to set the hook. As in

the coast or into Puget Sound. Mid-August is usually the earliest period the salmon may be taken with flies, since mature coho seem to be more prone to hit this gear. Coho flies resemble herring or candlefish, types of food fish salmon are feeding heavily upon before heading for spawning streams.

To locate coho in ocean waters fishermen should follow rips which gather bait. Trolling flies should be done on a zig-zag pattern with frequent changes of speed.

Cohos in ocean waters in September often average 10 pounds or better, with 15 and 18 pound salmon not uncommon. And that's a lot of scrappy fish on a fly with no sinker fouling up the detail.

But don't forget—hands in the pockets!

Catch That Clam!

Chief protection for razor clams is rapid movement. This comes as no surprise to those who have excavated sandy ocean beaches of the Northwest for the tasty shellfish. The clams have to move fast to escape crabs and man, their main enemies.

The four major razor clam beaches in Washington are Twin Harbors, Long Beach, Copalis and Mocrocks. There are over 50 miles of productive ocean beaches in these areas. Oregon's top razor clam beaches include Clatsop and several beaches between Newport and Florence. There is some razor clam digging at Cannon Beach and around Tillamook.

Best digging is in spring just before razor clams spawn. They are at their fattest during this period. Spawn ripens in the clam's digger or foot, and eggs and sperm are discharged into the open water. Fertilized eggs drift in the surf for six weeks before settling on the bottom and digging in. Natural mortality is great. This is compensated in part by the six to ten million eggs a female may develop each year.

Average length of 2-year-old razor clams is 4 to 4½ inches. Razor clams have a life expectancy of eight years.

Razor clams may be taken by either surf or dry digging. Spring and fall are best periods for surf digging, but diggers must be quick since the clams are in fluid sand along the water's edge. Good surf diggers bare clams with one swipe of the shovel, grabbing the neck immediately.

Inexperienced diggers will do best by dry digging.

Diggers should watch for clam sign or "shows" which are small dimples in the sand made when the clam withdraws his neck. Sometimes thumping the beach with a shovel handle or feet will cause razor clams to retract siphons with resultant dimple in the sand.

Best digging is usually on minus tides of about—two feet which allows around two hours of prime digging time.

Remove meat from shells by dropping clams in boiling water for a few seconds. In cleaning clams the gills and digestive tract are removed. These are the dark parts. An easy method to prepare razor clams for frying is to cut the tip of the neck off with scissors or a sharp knife, then open the body from the base of the foot to its end. The paired gills and palps which are now revealed are snipped off. The digger foot is squeezed and a cut is made to remove the gut. Then the digger is slit so that it will lie flat and the dark intestine is removed. Clams are rinsed and are ready for the pan.

Clams must be fried lightly and fast. They may be dipped in egg and then rolled in flour or meal before being dropped into a hot frying pan. They should be browned on both sides. Over-cooked razor clams are tough.

OCEAN ←

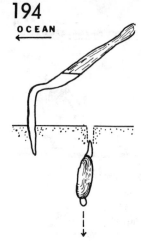

Digging razors can be frustrating until you get the hang of it. First, remember his back is to the ocean. ←

Don't Leave him alone on the sand after digging. Put him in the bucket. If not, he'll put his digger in and start for China. That's his neck out now. The digger on the other end is already opening and closing at work. →

Photos by Jim Stock

Drawings by Alaska Dept. Fish & Game

OCEAN ←

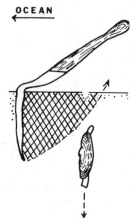

A couple minutes later, that clam has dug himself a starter. →

Take a quick swipe with the "gun" and lift out a chunk of sand right alongside the clam's hole. You may turn him up or bare his backside the first time—maybe the next. ←

Another minute or so and he's well on his way, going down. →

OCEAN ←

This picture of a clam half showing is only what you might reveal by hand digging after the first spade has been removed. If the shovel came this close, the thin shell would most likely be crushed. (And remember it's really "razor" cutting sharp!) ←

In a minute more that razor clam will have disappeared, his digger pulling him beneath the surface. Notice the siphon (neck) working. →

RAZOR CLAM BEACHES

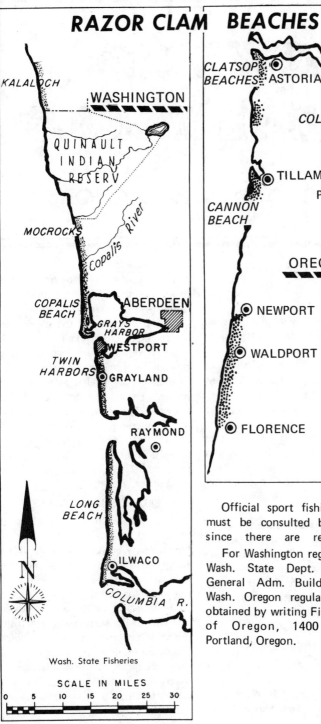

KALALOCH

WASHINGTON

QUINAULT INDIAN RESERV

Copalis River

MOCROCKS

COPALIS BEACH

ABERDEEN

GRAYS HARBOR

WESTPORT

TWIN HARBORS

GRAYLAND

RAYMOND

LONG BEACH

N

ILWACO

COLUMBIA R.

Wash. State Fisheries

SCALE IN MILES

0   5   10   15   20   25   30

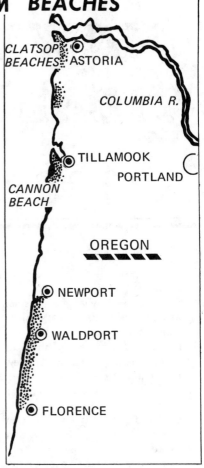

CLATSOP BEACHES

ASTORIA

COLUMBIA R.

TILLAMOOK

PORTLAND

CANNON BEACH

OREGON

NEWPORT

WALDPORT

FLORENCE

Official sport fishing regulations must be consulted before digging, since there are restrictions.

For Washington regulations write: Wash. State Dept. of Fisheries, General Adm. Building, Olympia, Wash. Oregon regulations may be obtained by writing Fish Commission of Oregon, 1400 S.W. Fifth, Portland, Oregon.

PROWL the TIDAL POOLS

By AL LASATER

Our diet and what we consider good to eat depends a great deal on custom and habit. We have in Northwest waters a number of seafoods that are eaten by very few people despite their excellent flavor and high nutritive value. In some cases people don't know that a particular organism is good, but in most cases are prejudiced in that seafoods which they are not accustomed to just don't look good to them. Actually, the proof is in the eating.

While Northwest residents dig and eat many clams, the horse clam is largely in disfavor. Part of this is due to the name, some to the need for more cleaning effort than is needed for steamer or butter clams, and much of it only because people have heard that they are not good.

TRY HORSE CLAMS

Horse clams are large and it doesn't take many to fill the average limit. Wash them off and cut the clam out of the shell. Often there are one or two small crabs inside the shell. They live there and don't make the clam less edible.

Cut the necks off the clams and freeze them. The necks have a rough outer covering which can be quite difficult to remove but when frozen they are easily peeled with a potato peeler. They may be ground for chowder, but are most delicious split open, pounded, and fried hot and quickly. The body of the clam may be split and the dark digestive gland removed. The body is good either fried or for chowder.

SMALL SNAILS TASTY

The marine snails that cling to rocks and pilings have a very fine flavor. Many are too small but those an inch and a half or more long have enough meat to be worthwhile. Boil the snails for about 15 minutes then cool enough so they can be handled. The part of the snail protruding from the shell has on it a round flat piece like a bit of plastic. Pull gently on this and most of the snails can be unscrewed from their shell. Bite the snail off close to your grip on the operculum and eat.

... much edible sea-food is overlooked

EAT 'EM RAW

The limpet is often called a "china hat" from its shape, and is found clinging to rocks. Those who like raw seafoods can eat them directly from the shell or when they are cut free from the shell they may be fried or made into a stew. When cut from the shell the inner area has a greenish mass which is perfectly good and should not be removed.

FRY CUCUMBERS QUICK

Sea cucumbers certainly do not look appetizing, with their sausage shape and red-brown warty skin, but this part isn't usually eaten anyway. Soon after capture they should be cut open from end to end and most of the internal organs will practically flow out. The inside of the body that is left has a thin muscle layer which is cut loose at one end and with care can be pulled loose from one end to the other. When removed the muscle will form a piece about the size of a man's thumb. Rinse these in salt water to remove the slime, pound them a bit to break the muscle and fry hot and quickly.

MORE RAW GOODIES

Sea urchins or sea biscuits, as they may be called, appeal to those who like raw seafoods. The green variety with the short spines is the one eaten. When the shell is broken open, the edible portion is the orange part. They are considered to be best during winter.

Squid and octopus are so widely eaten throughout the world that I hesitate to mention methods or recipes, knowing that I could not do justice to the wealth of information that exists. In addition, relatively few sport fishermen or beachcombers ever see them. If the fisherman does get a mess of squid or an octopus he need only inquire a bit and someone will come up with preparation and cooking methods.

WHY NOT PIONEER?

There are a number of other edible creatures and plants in the sea which are not only edible, but considered a delicacy by many people. Those who have a bit of the spirit of adventure and are not bound by habit and preconceived ideas can find some real rewards in good eating.

SAVE THE EGGS

There are many methods of preserving salmon or steelhead eggs for bait fishing. Some require special chemicals and considerable preparation time. While the more fussy techniques work fine, there's a simple way that produces fish-catching bait:

Separate layers of eggs in the skeins and rub powdered borax in thoroughly. Sprinkle and rub more borax over outside of the skeins.

Scissor thick egg skeins laterally

NO SMELL, LADIES

Wrap the skeins in absorbent paper towels, then in newspaper and place in refrigerator. (No, ladies—no smell with fresh eggs.) Length of time the eggs remain in the refrigerator depends on how juicy (mature) they are. Usually eggs taken from early-run steelhead require only one or two days, while ripe coho salmon eggs might take three or four days.

When some of the excess moisture has been absorbed by the paper towels and the eggs toughened, remove the skeins from the refrigerator. If skeins are large, cut them laterally with scissors, then cut eggs into bait-sized chunks over a pile or box of powdered borax. The baits should be rolled around or shaken in the box until completely covered with borax. Don't be stingy with the borax.

Cut eggs into bait-sized chunks.

FILL JARS FULL

Fill glass jars, such as peanut butter jars, to the brim with baits and sprinkle some borax over the top. Screw the lids on TIGHT.

Eggs prepared in this manner may be kept in refrigerators for about two weeks. When frozen they hold up to six months, but once thawed must be used within a week.

It is vital that POWDERED borax,

Roll baits in borax until all moisture is gone

not granular, be used. Grocers can order the powdered variety.

Anglers who prefer fresh eggs can stretch their egg supply by making "strawberries." This technique calls for maline cloth. (Light net material used on women's hats and available at dry goods stores) The material is cut into three or four inch squares, and bait-sized chunks are placed on each. The netting is pulled snug around the bait, gathered and tied at the top with thread.

The strawberries may be frozen and used at a later date. It is wise to place a piece of waxed paper between layers of baits for separation.

Advantage of this method is that baits last much longer.

Another variation involves sprinkling Sodium Sulfite, Merck No. 5201, over skeins or bait-sized chunks rather than using borax. Too heavy a layer will dry the eggs excessively. Eggs prepared in this manner milk well in the water.

MAKE SINGLE EGGS

It is possible for anglers to make their own single eggs if they want to go to the trouble. Skeins of mature eggs may be "singled" by gentle pressure over a screen large enough to permit eggs to drop through. The single eggs are placed in a thick saline solution (water and salt) capable of floating a chicken egg. The eggs (salmon, not chicken) are simmered until they are the correct consistency. This may be tested with a pin.

An old Indian trick is to strip loose eggs from a ripe female into a can, add a bit of river water, and place the can over the coals of a fire. When the eggs turn an opaque white they will stick on the hook. The word from the tribe is not to over-cook them.

Try Sturgeon

Both white and green sturgeon are taken by sport fishermen in Northwest waters. The Columbia river provides most of the fish. Oregon's Winchester Bay and lower reaches of the Rogue host sturgeon. In Washington such rivers as the Chehalis, Naselle and Willapa, in their tidewater reaches yield the fish.

White sturgeon are found in the Columbia. The greens prefer salt water.

WHITES ARE BIG

The whites are larger—up to 20 feet and 1800 pounds—and are considered better eating than the greens, which may reach 7 feet and 350 pounds. It is thought that the whites live part of their lives in the sea, ascending rivers to spawn. Some are land-locked in the upper Columbia.

Sturgeon are bottom feeders in fresh water, eating mollusks and crustaceans, along with smelt. The fish, which are representatives of an ancient group of fish, have a skeleton made up of cartilage. They grow very slowly, and probably do not reach spawning age until about 6 feet long, in the case of whites.

TAKEN ALL YEAR

Sturgeon may be caught on a year-around basis, but probably the best period is from late fall through early spring. Tackle must be stout—60 pound test line is common for bank fishermen, with 10 or 12 ounces of lead. Smelt or herring are used for bait. Fishing is done in deep holes, with the bait left to "soak" until a sturgeon picks it off the bottom. Ghost shrimp, in addition to smelt or herring, are used in tidal areas.

MEMBERS OF THE OREGON COAST CHARTERBOAT ASSOCIATION

PORT	BOAT NAME	NO. OF PASS.	LENGTH	SKIPPER/OWNER	BUSINESS PHONE NO.	HOME PHONE NO.	YEAR AROUND YES	NO	BOTTOM FISH	TUNA	SALMON	CHARTER OFFICE
ASTORIA	CHEYENNE	20	56	CLIFF THOMAS	325-7990	654-8964	X		X	X	X	ASTORIA THUNDERBIRD CHARTERS
ASTORIA	IRISH	20	53	KEN PETERSEN	325-7990	325-2607	X		X	X	X	ASTORIA THUNDERBIRD CHARTERS
ASTORIA	KINGFISHER	12	38	PAUL BRANHAM	325-7990	325-2390	X		X	X	X	ASTORIA THUNDERBIRD CHARTERS
ASTORIA	LIN-DEE	14	42	TONY FRANCISCONE	325-7990	292-0890	X		X	X	X	ASTORIA THUNDERBIRD CHARTERS
ASTORIA	SHAMROCK	15	44	GENE ITZEN	325-7990	325-5797		X	X	X	X	ASTORIA THUNDERBIRD CHARTERS
ASTORIA	SILVER FOX	12	38	LEE HUDSON	325-7990	472-6976	X		X	X	X	ASTORIA THUNDERBIRD CHARTERS
WARRENTON	AQUARIUS	6	34	DON BALDWIN - JIM HIER	861-3705	771-2967	X				X	AQUARIUS CHARTERS INC.
WARRENTON	DARK ROCK	6	32	GLEN BLACKSTONE	861-1445	244-1866	X		X		X	DARK ROCK CHARTERS INC.
WARRENTON	EXECUTIVE	6	32	FRED SCHMIDTKE	861-3705	861-1445	X		X	X	X	EXECUTIVE SALMON CHARTERS INC
WARRENTON	NAUGHTYLESS II	6	30	FRANK WARRENS	228-6607	245-0031	X				X	WARRENS AUTO & MARINE SRVC.
WARRENTON	OKIE	6	32	LEONARD MONTGOMERY	253-5186	253-5186	X				X	MONTY'S SALMON CHARTERS
WARRENTON	PACIFIC SALMON	12	40	BALDWIN/HIER/SCHMIDTKE	861-3705	861-1445	X		X	X	X	PACIFIC SALMON CHARTERS INC.
WARRENTON	ROCHELLE	6	31	ART BELLEUE	861-2221	254-4195	X		X	X	X	SKIPANON CHARTERS
WARRENTON	SEA PRIDE	15	45	A.F. "BUD" CHARLTON	861-2223	861-1233	X		X		X	WARRENTON DEEP SEA
HAMMOND	DOLL-FIN	15	38	HARLAN HAMEL	861-2698	861-2698		X	X	X	X	DOLL-FIN CHARTERS
HAMMOND	DONRIMIK	6	24	DON GILBERTSON	289-9578	289-9578		X	X	X	X	DON GILBERTSON CHARTERS
HAMMOND	MARTA	16	42	BOB WILKINS	861-1867	861-1867	X		X		X	PLAYTIME CHARTERS
HAMMOND	ROCKIN' C	6	33	EARL V. CADLE	861-1814	861-1814	X				X	KAMPER'S WEST KAMPGROUND
HAMMOND	STARR CHIEF	6	34	HAL STARR	861-1728	639-7870	X		X		X	TIKI CHARTERS
HAMMOND	SURF SCOOTER	15	43	RON LEITHIN	363-1343	371-9081	X		X	X	X	CURTION CHARTERS INC.
HAMMOND	TAKI TOOO	15	35	AL DEMMEL	861-1201	861-1201	X		X	X	X	TIKI CHARTERS
HAMMOND	TIME OUT	6	35	RAY ALT			X				X	SALMON SAFARI
HAMMOND	ZOFA	22	47	DOUGLAS YOUNG	861-1211	254-4670	X		X		X	FT. STEVENS SALMON CHARTERS
GARIBALDI	CHARLIE	24	50	DAVE HASS	322-3285	322-3389	X		X	X	X	SIGGI-G CHARTERS
GARIBALDI	D. & D. II	12	32	VERN BUELL	322-3666	322-3617	X		X	X	X	TROLLER'S CAFE & CHARTERS
GARIBALDI	FRAN-F	20	48	ED FISHER	322-3343	322-3343	X		X	X	X	DON OLSON CHARTERS
GARIBALDI	HARBORMASTER	16	46	DALE WALTERS	322-3395	322-3395	X		X	X	X	JOE'S DEEP SEA FISHING
GARIBALDI	KAZANI	6	38	ED BOUCHER	322-3666	322-3666	X		X	X	X	TROLLER'S CAFE & CHARTERS
GARIBALDI	KERRI-LINN	12	32	JON BROWN	322-3343	355-2439	X		X	X	X	DON OLSON CHARTERS
GARIBALDI	QUEEN OF HARTS	12	38	CLARE OLSON	322-3395	322-3252	X		X	X	X	DON OLSON CHARTERS
GARIBALDI	REEL-FUN	6	30	DON JOHNSON	322-3395	322-3395	X		X	X	X	JOE'S DEEP SEA FISHING
GARIBALDI	SCISSORBIL	6	34	MORRIE BARACKMAN	322-3285	322-3633	X		X	X	X	SIGGI-G CHARTERS
GARIBALDI	SIGGI-G	14	36	JOE GIERGA	322-3285	322-3285	X		X	X	X	SIGGI-G CHARTERS
DEPOE BAY	JIMCO	12	40	CHET GARDNER	765-2713	765-2713	X		X	X	X	JIMCO SPORTFISHING
DEPOE BAY	REGARD	14	42	BUD ROWANS	765-2673	765-2673	X		X	X	X	BUD ROWANS, INDEPENDENT
NEWPORT	ALLEGRA	6	36	W. WALKER LEROY	265-2673	265-2673		X	X	X	X	NEWPORT SPORTFISHING
NEWPORT	CHILOQUIN	14	40	H. STOCKMAN/R. CARLSON	265-7558	265-7558		X	X	X	X	NEWPORT SPORTFISHING
NEWPORT	FRIENDSHIP	6	38	RALPH WONSYLD	265-7558	265-7558	X		X	X	X	NEWPORT SPORTFISHING
NEWPORT	KAI-AKU	14	38	STEVE BOND	265-7558	265-7558	X		X	X	X	NEWPORT SPORTFISHING
NEWPORT	TAKU	16	50	WALT MARCHEL	265-7558	265-7558	X		X	X	X	NEWPORT SPORTFISHING
NEWPORT	SEA VENTURE I	30	50	BURT WADDELL	265-2101	265-2101	X		X	X	X	NEWPORT TRADEWINDS
NEWPORT	WHITE SWAN III	8	35	MIKE MORGAN	265-7441	265-7441	X		X	X	X	SEA GULL CHARTERS
WINCHESTER BAY	SHAMROCK II	6	35	NORVAL SHANNON	271-3232	271-3232		X	X	X	X	SHAMROCK CHARTERS
COOS BAY	MR. KAY	10	42	FREEMAN KELLY	888-4139	888-4139		X	X	X	X	B. & B. CHARTERS INC.
BROOKINGS	LETA "J"	15	40	FRED STUTSMAN	469-3452	469-3301		X	X	X	X	SPORTHAVEN MARINA